Muhamma Jinnah: The Leader of Pakistan

CW00543031

Copyright

Published by Azhar ul Haque Sario
azhar.sario@hotmail.co.uk

Table of Contents

Book Map

Chapter 1: The Beginning

Here, we start our journey into the life of Muhammad Ali Jinnah, the architect of Pakistan. Imagine a man whose vision and determination changed the map of the world. This chapter gives you a sneak peek into his extraordinary life, highlighting the big moments and key themes we'll dive into.

Chapter 2: Roots and Childhood

Think of a tree and its deep roots. This chapter is all about Jinnah's roots - his family, where he came from, and his early years. We'll explore the world he grew up in and the experiences that started to shape this future leader as a young boy.

Chapter 3: From Courtrooms to Politics

Jinnah's story isn't just political; it starts in courtrooms. We'll see how a young lawyer's sharp mind set the stage for his political journey. It's a tale of ambition, learning, and the first steps towards a grander stage.

Chapter 4: In the Congress Corridors

Imagine Jinnah in the bustling halls of the Indian National Congress, working towards Hindu-Muslim unity. But, not all stories have happy endings. We'll see how his dreams began to clash with reality, leading to a change in his path.

Chapter 5: Champion for Muslim Rights

Now, picture Jinnah as a voice for the unheard. This chapter talks about how he stood up for Muslim rights and began dreaming of a separate nation. It's about ideas, hopes, and the birth of a vision.

Chapter 6: Leading the League
Here, Jinnah takes center stage in the All-India Muslim League. It's a story of leadership, challenges, and the quest for a homeland. We'll witness the struggles and triumphs of a leader in the making.

Chapter 7: The Lahore Resolution and Beyond
Imagine a historic resolution that sets a nation's destiny. This chapter covers the passion, the people, and the politics behind the Lahore Resolution and the Pakistan Movement. It's about uniting different voices under one dream.

Chapter 8: The Art of Negotiation
Dive into the complex world of political negotiations. Jinnah, the British, and the Congress - it's a high-stakes game that decides the fate of millions. We'll unravel the twists and turns that led to the creation of two nations.

Chapter 9: A Nation is Born
The birth of Pakistan – a moment in history. This chapter captures the drama, the challenges, and Jinnah's leadership in carving out a new country. It's a tumultuous yet triumphant tale of nation-building.

Chapter 10: The Founding Father
Here, we celebrate Jinnah as Pakistan's founding father. From setting up a government to envisioning a future, it's about the early steps of a newborn nation and the man leading the charge.

Chapter 11: Shaping a Country
Think of a sculptor shaping clay. This chapter is about Jinnah shaping Pakistan's constitution and governance. It's a journey through debates, decisions, and the challenges of a country in its infancy.

Chapter 12: A Leader's Legacy
What makes a great leader? This chapter looks at Jinnah's leadership style, his political thoughts, and the lasting impact he made on Pakistan. It's a reflection on what it means to lead.

Chapter 13: The Man Behind the Leader
Every leader has a personal side. Here, we peek into Jinnah's personal life, his family, and the relationships that shaped him. It's about the human side of a national icon.

Chapter 14: Dreams for Tomorrow
What did Jinnah dream for Pakistan's future? This chapter talks about his hopes and plans for the nation's progress. It's a glimpse into a leader's vision for the road ahead.

Chapter 15: Ideological Footprints
Jinnah's ideas didn't just shape a nation; they shaped its society and culture. Here, we explore how his legacy influences debates on identity, citizenship, and governance in Pakistan today.

Chapter 16: A Global Perspective
Jinnah on the world stage – it's about his international impact and how he presented Pakistan to the world. This chapter shows a leader's role in global diplomacy and international relations.

Chapter 17: Remembering Jinnah
How do you remember a legend? This chapter is all about how Pakistan and the world commemorate Jinnah's legacy. It's a celebration of a national hero and his lasting symbol.

Chapter 18: Still Relevant
Decades later, Jinnah's influence lingers in modern Pakistan. This chapter reflects on his enduring relevance, his ideas, and how they continue to inspire and provoke thought about Pakistan's future.

Chapter 19: Revisiting the Legacy
No story is without its critiques. In this final chapter, we take a balanced look at Jinnah's legacy, exploring the debates and controversies that surround this monumental figure in history.

Azhar ul Haque Sario

Introduction

Muhammad Ali Jinnah, a man of great vision and remarkable leadership, holds a pivotal place in the history of Pakistan. Born on December 25, 1876, in Karachi, then part of British-ruled India, Jinnah's journey from a young barrister to the founder of Pakistan is a tale of relentless struggle, astute politics, and unwavering determination. His life and legacy are intricately woven into the fabric of Pakistan's history, making him an enduring symbol of pride and inspiration for the nation.

Early Life and Education
Jinnah's early life set the foundation for his future achievements. He received his primary education in Karachi before moving to Bombay for further studies. His journey to London to study law was a turning point. There, he was exposed to the ideas of freedom, democracy, and self-rule. His time in Britain significantly shaped his political views and strategies.

Legal Career and Entry into Politics
After returning to India, Jinnah quickly made a name for himself as a brilliant lawyer. His entry into politics was marked by his joining the Indian National Congress in 1906. Initially, he believed in Hindu-Muslim unity in the struggle for independence from British rule. His eloquence, clear vision, and legal acumen made him a prominent figure in India's political landscape.

Shift to Muslim League and Vision for Pakistan
His vision for a separate nation for Muslims began to take shape amidst growing communal tensions and the fear of Muslim interests being overshadowed in an independent but Hindu-majority India.

The Lahore Resolution and the Demand for Pakistan

The Lahore Resolution in 1940, spearheaded by Jinnah, was a landmark moment. It formally presented the demand for a separate Muslim state, later to be named Pakistan. Jinnah's leadership was instrumental in galvanizing support for this idea among Muslims across British India.

Struggle for Independence
Jinnah's unwavering stance and skilled negotiations in the face of British resistance and Hindu-Muslim tensions were pivotal in the creation of Pakistan. His strategy was marked by legal prowess, political acumen, and the ability to maintain unity among diverse Muslim groups. His slogan, "Unity, Faith, Discipline," became the rallying cry for Muslims striving for an independent homeland.

The Creation of Pakistan
On August 14, 1947, Pakistan emerged on the world map as a sovereign state, predominantly for Muslims of the Indian subcontinent. This was the culmination of Jinnah's tireless efforts and a testament to his leadership. He became the country's first Governor-General, steering the nascent nation through the initial, tumultuous years.

Jinnah's Vision for Pakistan
Jinnah envisioned Pakistan as a progressive, democratic, and inclusive state where all citizens, regardless of religion or ethnicity, could live in harmony. He advocated for women's rights, minority protection, and a forward-looking socio-economic framework. His speeches often emphasized justice, fair play, and equality.

Legacy and Challenges

Jinnah's death on September 11, 1948, just a year after Pakistan's creation, was a significant blow to the young nation. The ideals and principles he stood for remain a guiding light for Pakistan. However, the challenges he foresaw – sectarianism, regional disparities, and governance issues – have continued to affect the country.

Jinnah's Influence on Modern Pakistan

Today, Jinnah's influence in Pakistan is ubiquitous. He is revered as the 'Father of the Nation,' and his birthday is a national holiday. His portraits adorn government offices, public spaces, and educational institutions. His speeches and writings are taught in schools, serving as a reminder of his vision and ideals.

Chapter 2: Ancestry and Early Life

Jinnah's family background

Muhammad Ali Jinnah, the founder of Pakistan, is a figure of immense historical significance. His journey from a young boy to the leader of a nation is intertwined with a rich family background, ancestral roots, and cultural heritage. This exploration will delve deep into these aspects of his life, painting a vivid picture of the man who played a pivotal role in shaping the destiny of millions.

1. Family Background
Born on December 25, 1876, in Karachi, which was then part of British India, Muhammad Ali Jinnah came from a family that was not extraordinarily affluent but held a respectable position in society. His father, Jinnah Poonja, was a successful merchant with a background that combined a blend of Gujarati and Khoja cultures. This mix played a crucial role in shaping the environment in which Jinnah grew up.

The family belonged to the Khoja Muslim community, which followed the Shia Ismaili sect of Islam under the spiritual leadership of the Aga Khan. However, Jinnah later chose to adopt the Sunni Muslim faith, a decision that was personal and reflected his individual beliefs.

Jinnah was the second child of his parents, Poonja and Mithibai. His siblings, including his brothers and sisters, were part of a large family, typical of that era. The familial environment was traditional, yet it allowed for modern and liberal ideas, which were slowly seeping into the Indian subcontinent during the British Raj.

2. Ancestral Roots

Jinnah's ancestry can be traced back to the 19th century in Gujarat, India. His paternal grandfather, Premjibhai Meghji Thakkar, was a Hindu Rajput who converted to Islam and joined the Khoja community. This conversion was not just a change of religion but also a step into a new cultural and social milieu.

The Khoja community itself had an interesting history. Originally Hindus, they were converted to Nizari Ismailism under the persuasion of Islamic missionaries. This background gave Jinnah's family a unique standing – one foot in the deep-rooted traditions of the Indian subcontinent and the other in the evolving landscape of Islamic culture and British influence.

Jinnah's father, Jinnah Poonja, was born in Paneli village in the Gondal state of Kathiawar and later moved to Karachi for business, where Jinnah was born. This move from a small village to a bustling port city was a significant shift that brought the family into the heart of the colonial economic and cultural exchange.

3. Cultural Heritage

The cultural heritage that Jinnah inherited was a tapestry of Indian, Islamic, and British influences. Growing up in Karachi, a cosmopolitan center, he was exposed to diverse cultures and ideas from a young age. This exposure played a crucial role in shaping his secular views and political ideology.

Jinnah's education in Karachi and later in London further broadened his horizons. He adopted Western styles of dress and mannerisms, and his time in Britain had a profound impact on his legal and political thinking. However, he never lost touch with his roots, often reflecting a deep understanding and appreciation of Indian culture and history.

The cultural diversity of his family background and upbringing was evident in his political career. Jinnah was initially a staunch supporter of Hindu-Muslim unity in India. His efforts in this direction reflected his belief in a multicultural society where different religious and ethnic groups could coexist harmoniously.

As a leader, Jinnah's approach was marked by his upbringing in a family that straddled different worlds. He was adept at navigating the complexities of Indian politics, which was deeply influenced by religious and cultural factors. His ability to reconcile his Westernized outlook with his deep understanding of Indian society was one of his greatest strengths.

Account of Jinnah's early life

Muhammad Ali Jinnah, a pivotal figure in the history of South Asia, was born on December 25, 1876, in Karachi, which was then part of British India and is now in Pakistan. His life's journey, from an early age to becoming the founder of Pakistan, is a tale of determination, vision, and leadership. In this detailed account, we will explore his early life, upbringing, education, and the formative experiences that shaped his character and worldview, spread over five distinct sections.

1. Early Life
Jinnah was born into a Gujarati Muslim family. His father, Jinnah Poonja, was a prosperous merchant. The family belonged to the Ismaili Khoja community, followers of the Aga Khan. His early life in Karachi exposed him to diverse cultural and religious influences, which played a crucial role in shaping his inclusive perspective later in life.

Karachi, a cosmopolitan port city, was bustling with different communities and cultures during Jinnah's childhood. Growing up in this environment, Jinnah developed a broad outlook, interacting with people from various backgrounds. This exposure was significant in forming his secular views.

2. Upbringing
Jinnah's upbringing was steeped in a mix of traditional and modern influences. His father, being a merchant, emphasized the importance of education and business acumen. The family environment was liberal for that era, allowing Jinnah to grow up with a sense of independence and self-reliance.

His mother, Mithibai, played a vital role in his upbringing. Her influence ensured that Jinnah was grounded in his cultural and religious roots, yet open to modern ideas. The values of honesty, integrity, and discipline were deeply ingrained in him from a young age.

3. Education
Jinnah's formal education began at the Sindh Madrasatul Islam in Karachi, which combined traditional Islamic education with modern subjects. His early schooling laid the foundation for his fluency in English and his interest in legal and political matters.

At the age of 16, Jinnah traveled to London to join a commercial firm. However, his interest soon shifted to law. He enrolled at Lincoln's Inn, one of the prestigious Inns of Court in London, to pursue legal studies. His time in London was transformative. The exposure to British political and legal systems, as well as Western ideas of democracy and justice, deeply influenced his thinking.

During his stay in London, Jinnah also came across the works of British political thinkers, which further shaped his political views. His attire, language, and lifestyle underwent a significant transformation, reflecting a blend of Eastern values and Western liberalism.

4. Character Formation
Jinnah's character was a blend of resolute determination and a pragmatic approach to issues. His time in London was crucial in this regard. He developed a keen sense of justice and fairness, along with an appreciation for the rule of law. These attributes became the cornerstone of his political career.

His experiences, both in Karachi and London, instilled in him a strong sense of self-identity and purpose. Jinnah was known for his integrity, discipline, and dedication. These traits were evident in his legal career, where he gained a reputation for his sharp mind and eloquent oratory.

5. Worldview Development

Jinnah's worldview was shaped by a combination of his upbringing in a diverse city like Karachi, his education, and his experiences in Britain. He believed in the ideals of democracy, equality, and justice. His time in Europe coincided with the period of the Indian independence movement, which influenced his political ideals.

Upon returning to India, Jinnah initially worked as a lawyer but soon became involved in politics. His early political stance was moderate, advocating for Hindu-Muslim unity and constitutional reforms within the British Indian Empire. However, his experiences with political realities in India, especially concerning communal tensions and the struggle for independence, led him to advocate for a separate Muslim state, leading to the creation of Pakistan.

Chapter 3: Legal Career and Political Awakening

Entry into the legal profession

Muhammad Ali Jinnah, a pivotal figure in South Asian history, particularly in the creation of Pakistan, had an extensive and multifaceted career. Before he emerged as a leader who would guide the formation of a new nation, Jinnah traversed a significant journey in the legal profession. His early experiences as a lawyer shaped not only his professional outlook but also his approach to politics and leadership. This exploration into Jinnah's entry into the legal profession and his initial experiences as a lawyer sheds light on how these formative years impacted his later life and the path to Pakistan's independence.

Entry into the Legal Profession
In London, Jinnah joined Lincoln's Inn, one of the four Inns of Court in London, to train as a barrister. This decision was influenced by a desire to understand the legal underpinnings of the British Empire, which then governed India. His choice of Lincoln's Inn is often attributed to a plaque at the entrance listing the names of the world's greatest lawgivers, including Prophet Muhammad. Jinnah saw law as a tool to bring about change and as a profession that commanded respect.

While in London, Jinnah also immersed himself in the political and cultural life of the city. He attended theatre performances, closely followed political debates, and became acquainted with the works of British political thinkers. This period was crucial in shaping his political views, which later played a significant role in his leadership in India.

Return to India and Early Legal Career

Jinnah returned to India in 1896 and began his legal career in Bombay, now Mumbai. His initial years were challenging, as he struggled to establish himself in the competitive legal environment of Bombay. He initially took up work as a clerk to a barrister and also taught English at a local school to support himself. His first legal case was a petition at a small causes court, where he was so nervous that he could not speak and eventually offered the brief to a colleague.

Despite this rocky start, Jinnah's persistence and dedication soon paid off. His meticulousness, sharp legal acumen, and ability to present clear and cogent arguments began to earn him recognition. He gained experience in various legal matters, ranging from commercial litigation to criminal defense. One of his significant early cases was the 1908 Pherozeshah Mehta's case, which brought him into the limelight. His handling of this case showcased his skills in interpreting legal texts and constructing persuasive arguments.

Building Reputation as a Lawyer

Jinnah's reputation as a lawyer grew rapidly. His practice extended to cases involving constitutional law, a field that later became instrumental in his political career. He was known for his eloquent oratory, incisive legal knowledge, and unwavering commitment to his clients. These traits not only brought him professional success but also respect among his peers and the public.

In 1906, Jinnah represented Bal Gangadhar Tilak, a prominent leader of the Indian National Congress, in a sedition case. Although Jinnah lost the case, his defense was praised for its brilliance and depth. This case was a turning point, marking Jinnah's entry into the political arena of India.

Impact of Legal Career on Political Life
Jinnah's legal career significantly influenced his political approach. His legal training provided him with a framework for understanding and interpreting the law and governance. He applied these skills in his political endeavors, advocating for constitutional methods and legal frameworks for achieving political goals.

His legal background also influenced his advocacy for minority rights, which later became a cornerstone of his political ideology in fighting for a separate nation for Muslims in India. He approached the complex issue of Hindu-Muslim unity and the demand for Pakistan with a legalistic and pragmatic mindset, shaped by his years of legal practice.

Political awakening

Muhammad Ali Jinnah, a key figure in the history of South Asia, played an instrumental role in the creation of Pakistan. His journey from being a young barrister to becoming the founder of a nation is marked by various events and influences that shaped his political awakening and early involvement in Indian nationalist politics. To understand his transformation and his early political journey, it is essential to delve into the background and influences that shaped his vision and actions.

Influence of Western Education
Jinnah's Western education was a significant factor in his political awakening. The exposure to British political thought, the parliamentary system, and the ideals of the Enlightenment played a considerable role in shaping his early political views. He was particularly influenced by the concepts of rule of law and equal rights, which later became central to his political ideology.

Return to India and Early Career
Upon returning to India in 1896, Jinnah started his legal practice in Bombay. However, it was the political milieu of India that gradually drew him into the realm of politics. The Indian National Congress (INC), at that time, was increasingly becoming a platform for voicing Indian aspirations against British rule.

Entry into Politics
Jinnah's entry into politics was marked by his joining the Indian National Congress in 1906. This decision was influenced by the growing discontent among Indians regarding British policies and the rising demand

for greater self-governance. Jinnah, with his legal background and modernist views, found the platform of the INC conducive for his political initiation.

Role in Congress and Moderate Approach
Initially, Jinnah was part of the moderate faction within the Congress. He believed in constitutional methods and legal frameworks to achieve political goals. His approach was marked by a belief in gradual reform rather than immediate independence from British rule. This period saw Jinnah advocating for Indian representation in government bodies and the legal system.

Influence of Contemporary Leaders
Jinnah was influenced by several contemporary leaders. Figures like Dadabhai Naoroji, known as the Grand Old Man of India, and Gopal Krishna Gokhale, a senior leader of the Congress, played a part in shaping his political thought. Their moderate approach towards gaining self-governance influenced Jinnah's early political strategy.

Shift in Perspective
Over time, Jinnah's views evolved. The slow pace of reforms and the apparent reluctance of the British to grant substantial self-governance led to a change in his perspective. The events like the partition of Bengal in 1905 and the subsequent rise of extremist voices within the Congress made Jinnah reassess his moderate stance.

Involvement in Muslim Politics
Jinnah's involvement in Muslim politics started as he became more concerned about the political rights and representation of Muslims in India. He joined the All-India Muslim League in 1913, which marked a

significant turn in his political journey. His role in the
League was instrumental in articulating the political
aspirations of Indian Muslims.

Balancing Nationalist and Communal Concerns
One of the critical aspects of Jinnah's early political
career was his effort to balance nationalist aspirations
with communal concerns. He worked towards Hindu-
Muslim unity, believing that a collaborative approach
was vital for the political advancement of Indians. The
Lucknow Pact of 1916, where the Congress and the
Muslim League agreed on a formula for representation,
was a significant achievement in this regard.

Political Awakening: A Confluence of Influences
Jinnah's political awakening was not a sudden event but
a gradual process influenced by a confluence of factors.
His education, early legal career, exposure to Western
ideals, the political environment of India, and the
influence of contemporary leaders all played a part. His
initial involvement in Indian nationalist politics was
marked by a moderate approach, gradually evolving as
he became more involved in the complexities of Indian
politics.

Chapter 4: Leadership in the Indian National Congress

Role within the Indian National Congress

Muhammad Ali Jinnah, a pivotal figure in the history of South Asia, played a significant role in the Indian National Congress before founding Pakistan. His journey with the Congress is a tale of evolving political ideologies and a testament to his dynamic leadership.

Early Involvement in the Congress
Jinnah's political journey began in the early 20th century when he joined the Indian National Congress. At this time, the Congress was the primary political organization opposing British rule in India. Jinnah, a barrister by profession, brought with him a unique blend of Western education and deep understanding of Indian issues. He was initially a moderate in his political approach, advocating for constitutional methods to achieve political reform.

Advocacy for Hindu-Muslim Unity
One of Jinnah's early significant contributions was his strong advocacy for Hindu-Muslim unity. He believed that a united front of Hindus and Muslims was essential for effective opposition against British colonialism. Jinnah worked closely with prominent Congress leaders like Gopal Krishna Gokhale, who influenced his moderate political stance.

Role in Home Rule Movement
During the Home Rule Movement, which sought self-governance for India, Jinnah played an influential role. He was a part of the movement's leadership, aligning with leaders like Annie Besant and Bal Gangadhar Tilak. Jinnah's involvement in this movement reflected his dedication to India's self-governance and his ability to work across different political ideologies.

Disillusionment and Shift in Ideology
Over time, Jinnah became disillusioned with the Congress, primarily due to the growing influence of Mohandas Karamchand Gandhi. Gandhi's methods and ideology, particularly the emphasis on mass protests and non-cooperation, were in stark contrast to Jinnah's constitutional and legalistic approach. This divergence led to Jinnah's gradual distancing from the Congress.

The Lucknow Pact
Before his estrangement from the Congress, Jinnah played a key role in the Lucknow Pact of 1916, an agreement between the Congress and the All-India Muslim League, of which Jinnah was also a member. This pact was a significant achievement in Indian politics, as it presented a united front of Hindu and Muslim communities seeking constitutional reforms. Jinnah was hailed as the "Ambassador of Hindu-Muslim Unity" during this period.

Transition towards Muslim League Leadership
As communal tensions in India escalated, Jinnah's emphasis shifted towards addressing the concerns of the Muslim community. His growing belief in the need for a separate Muslim nation led to his increased involvement with the Muslim League. This shift

marked the beginning of his journey towards becoming the chief architect of Pakistan.

Legacy in Congress and Beyond
Jinnah's time in the Indian National Congress is a remarkable chapter in his political life. It showcases his initial commitment to a united, independent India and his gradual transformation into a leader who sought a separate nation for Muslims. This transformation was driven by his changing perspective on Hindu-Muslim relations, the effectiveness of Congress's strategies against British rule, and his vision for the Muslim community in a post-colonial India.

Jinnah's legacy in the Congress is complex. While he initially contributed significantly to the Congress's efforts for Indian independence, his eventual ideological shift led him to pursue a different path, culminating in the creation of Pakistan. His journey within the Congress reflects the political and communal complexities of the Indian independence movement.

Early efforts towards Hindu-Muslim unity

Muhammad Ali Jinnah, a name synonymous with the creation and foundation of Pakistan, was a towering figure in South Asian history. His journey from a young Bombay lawyer to the leader of the All-India Muslim League and eventually the founder of Pakistan is a story of political acumen, dedication, and vision. Among the many facets of his multifaceted life, one of the most significant was his early efforts towards fostering Hindu-Muslim unity, a period often overshadowed by his later role in partitioning India.

In the early 1900s, India was a tapestry of diverse cultures, languages, and religions under British colonial rule. The Indian National Congress was the primary political vehicle for Indian nationalism, advocating for self-rule. Jinnah, who joined the Congress in 1906, initially aligned with its moderate faction. His eloquence, sharp legal mind, and commitment to constitutional methods made him a notable figure in the party.

Jinnah's belief in Hindu-Muslim unity was evident in his opposition to the partition of Bengal in 1905, a move by the British that was seen as an attempt to divide and rule by splitting the region on religious lines. He worked alongside prominent Congress leaders like Gopal Krishna Gokhale, advocating for a united front against the British.

The Lucknow Pact of 1916 was a landmark in Jinnah's career and a high point in Hindu-Muslim relations. Jinnah played a key role in brokering this agreement between the Congress and the All-India Muslim League, of which he was also a member. The pact was a mutual arrangement for the two communities to work together for constitutional reforms. This was a significant achievement, as it brought the League, which had been founded in 1906 to protect Muslim interests, into a closer relationship with the Congress.

During this period, Jinnah was often referred to as the "Ambassador of Hindu-Muslim Unity," a title given to him by Sarojini Naidu, a prominent Congress leader and poet. His efforts were primarily focused on ensuring that both communities could coexist and cooperate within the framework of a single nation. He believed that constitutional and political advancements could be achieved faster if Hindus and Muslims presented a united front.

However, the landscape of Indian politics was changing rapidly. The aftermath of World War I, the rise of Mahatma Gandhi, and the shift towards mass politics and non-cooperation movements began to alter the dynamics of the Indian freedom struggle. Gandhi's methods, which were distinctly different from the constitutionalist approach of Jinnah, began to gain more traction among the masses. This period saw the rise of more vocal demands for independence and an increased focus on direct action and civil disobedience.

Jinnah's discomfort with these methods led to a gradual distancing from the Congress. He was increasingly seen as a voice for moderate, constitutional politics, which was losing ground to the more radical approaches championed by Gandhi and others. This divergence marked the beginning of a shift in Jinnah's political journey, which would later lead him to demand a separate nation for Muslims.

The decline of Hindu-Muslim unity in the 1920s was marked by events like the Khilafat movement, which Jinnah criticized, and the increasing communalization of politics. The seeds of division, sown by various political and social developments, began to grow. Jinnah's disillusionment with the Congress and his evolving view of Muslim nationalism laid the foundation for his later advocacy for Pakistan.

In retrospect, Jinnah's early efforts towards Hindu-Muslim unity highlight a complex and dynamic era in Indian history. His initial vision of a united India, where Hindus and Muslims could work together for common goals, gradually gave way to a realization that the political and social realities of India might necessitate a different approach for safeguarding Muslim interests.

Jinnah's journey from an ambassador of unity to the proponent of a separate Muslim nation is a testament to the intricate and often conflicting currents of history. His early years, marked by a firm belief in collaboration and coexistence, stand in stark contrast to his later stance, underscoring the transformative nature of his political life and the tumultuous times in which he lived.

This transformation of Jinnah's political ideology, from a unifier to a divider, is a crucial chapter in the history of South Asia. It speaks volumes about the complexities of colonial politics, the challenges of accommodating diverse religious and cultural identities, and the sometimes-unpredictable nature of political journeys.

Disillusionment with the Congress

Muhammad Ali Jinnah, the founder of Pakistan, is a towering figure in the history of South Asia. His journey from being a member of the Indian National Congress to becoming the leader of the All-India Muslim League and the driving force behind the creation of Pakistan is a tale of political evolution, ideological shifts, and response to the changing socio-political landscape of India under British rule. To understand this transformation, it is crucial to explore the factors that led to Jinnah's disillusionment with the Congress and his subsequent estrangement from the party.

Early Political Involvement and Congress
Jinnah's political journey began with his involvement in the Indian National Congress. Initially, he was an ardent supporter of Hindu-Muslim unity and believed in the Congress's secular and inclusive ideology. His vision was for a united India where all communities could coexist in harmony. Jinnah's eloquence, legal acumen, and commitment to constitutional methods earned him respect across the political spectrum.

Factors Leading to Disillusionment with Congress
Rising Communal Tensions: The early 20th century witnessed an increase in communal tensions in India. These tensions were exacerbated by the British policy of divide and rule, which aimed to create divisions between Hindus and Muslims. Jinnah, who championed secularism, found this environment increasingly challenging.

Hindu Mahasabha Influence in Congress: The rise of Hindu nationalist groups like the Hindu Mahasabha

34

within the Congress and their influence on its policies and direction was a significant concern for Jinnah. He feared that the Congress was becoming more a vehicle for Hindu interests than a truly national party representing all Indians.

Lack of Representation for Muslims: Jinnah began to feel that the Congress was not adequately representing the interests of the Muslim community. He argued for separate electorates for Muslims to ensure their political representation, but this was not fully supported by the Congress leadership.

Nehru Report: The Nehru Report of 1928, a response to the British challenge to Indians to propose a constitution for themselves, was a turning point. The report did not meet the demands of the Muslim League, led by Jinnah at the time, for proportional representation and the protection of Muslim political rights.

Personal Rifts: Jinnah's relations with key Congress leaders, especially Jawaharlal Nehru and Mahatma Gandhi, became strained. He disagreed with Gandhi's methods of mass mobilization and non-cooperation, preferring constitutional methods and negotiation.

The Turning Point: From Congress to Muslim League Jinnah's growing disillusionment with the Congress culminated in his decision to embrace the cause of Muslim nationalism. This was not an overnight transformation but a gradual process influenced by the political and communal developments of the time.

The Lahore Resolution (1940): The Lahore Resolution of 1940, passed by the All-India Muslim League, called for independent states for Muslims in the northwestern and eastern areas of India. This was a radical departure from Jinnah's earlier stance and marked his complete estrangement from the Congress.

World War II and Political Developments: The period of World War II saw significant political developments in India. The British government's decision to involve India in the war without consulting Indian leaders, the Quit India Movement by the Congress, and the consequent crackdown on Congress leaders provided Jinnah and the Muslim League with an opportunity to assert their demands more forcefully.

Jinnah's Vision of Pakistan: Jinnah's vision of Pakistan evolved as a response to his belief that Muslims would not be able to practice their religion freely and live with dignity in a Hindu-dominated India. He saw the creation of Pakistan as the only solution to safeguard the rights and identity of Muslims.

Conclusion
Muhammad Ali Jinnah's journey from a Congress leader to the founder of Pakistan was marked by a complex interplay of personal beliefs, political ideologies, and the turbulent events of his time. His disillusionment with the Congress was not merely a result of personal differences but stemmed from deeper concerns about the representation and rights of Muslims in a predominantly Hindu India. The shift in Jinnah's political stance reflects the dynamic nature of the subcontinent's political landscape in the first half of the 20th century. His legacy, therefore, is not just about the creation of a new nation but also about the struggle for minority rights and the challenges of building a nation amidst deep-seated communal divides.

Chapter 5: Advocacy for Muslim Rights

Advocacy for the rights of Muslims in British India

Muhammad Ali Jinnah's role in advocating for the rights of Muslims in British India was pivotal and complex. His early political career saw him rise to prominence within the Indian National Congress, where he initially championed Hindu-Muslim unity. This period was marked by his involvement in shaping the 1916 Lucknow Pact, which was a significant agreement between the Congress and the All-India Muslim League, aimed at presenting a united front to the British for self-governance in India. However, Jinnah's views evolved over time, particularly after 1920 when he resigned from the Congress due to its endorsement of satyagraha, a form of nonviolent resistance that he considered akin to political anarchy.

Jinnah's advocacy for Muslim rights became increasingly focused as he led the All-India Muslim League. By 1940, he had become a staunch supporter of the idea that Muslims should have their own state to prevent potential marginalization in a Hindu-majority independent India. This led to the Lahore Resolution in 1940, which demanded a separate nation for Indian Muslims. The Muslim League under Jinnah's leadership gained considerable strength during World War II, and in the provincial elections held shortly after the war, it won the majority of seats reserved for Muslims.

Jinnah's efforts culminated in the creation of Pakistan, where he served as the first governor-general. His vision for Pakistan was anchored in modern democratic principles, constitutionalism, civil and political rights, the rule of law, and equal citizenship for all, irrespective of religion, caste, or region. He imagined a nation where all citizens would be treated equally under the constitution and law, as he articulated in his address to the Constituent Assembly on August 11, 1947.

However, the path Pakistan took after Jinnah's death diverged significantly from his vision. During the military regime of General Zia-ul-Haq, Pakistan underwent a period of Islamization, which reinterpreted Jinnah's use of Islamic idiom and discourse to justify a more orthodox and conservative religious political order. This was a departure from Jinnah's initial moderate approach to integrating Islam into the state's identity.

Throughout his political journey, Jinnah's strategies and orientations were influenced by multiple factors, including his exposure to British liberalism during his studies in London, his legal background, and his experiences with the Congress Party and British colonial policies. These experiences shaped his evolving views on the political and constitutional rights of Muslims within the Indian subcontinent.

In summary, Jinnah's advocacy for Muslim rights in British India was characterized by a transition from promoting Hindu-Muslim unity to championing the cause of a separate Muslim nation, driven by his concerns over the political and social status of Muslims in a post-independence Indian subcontinent. His vision for Pakistan was rooted in democratic ideals and equality, although the trajectory of the nation post-independence diverged from these principles.

Evolving vision for a separate Muslim state

Muhammad Ali Jinnah, renowned as the founding father of Pakistan, is a figure of monumental importance in South Asian history. His journey from a proponent of Hindu-Muslim unity to the architect of a separate Muslim state is a tale of political evolution, driven by the tides of historical events, personal convictions, and the complex socio-political landscape of British India. This analysis delves into the various facets of Jinnah's vision, examining the shifts and developments in his thought process that ultimately led to the creation of Pakistan.

Gradual Shift Towards Muslim Nationalism
The turning point in Jinnah's political journey came with the deepening divide between the Hindu and Muslim communities. Factors contributing to this shift included:

The Rise of Communal Politics: The early 20th century witnessed a rise in communal tensions in India. Organizations like the Hindu Mahasabha began to emerge, advocating for Hindu interests, which alarmed the Muslim community.

Congress Policies: The policies and actions of the Congress, perceived as favoring Hindu interests, contributed to Jinnah's disillusionment. The Congress's decision to not form coalition governments with the All-India Muslim League in provinces where the League had won considerable seats in the 1937 elections was a critical moment.

Personal Experiences: Jinnah's experiences with Congress leaders, especially his disagreements with Mahatma Gandhi and Jawaharlal Nehru, played a significant role. He felt that their approaches were marginalizing Muslim voices in Indian politics.

The Lahore Resolution and the Demand for Pakistan
Jinnah's transformation reached its zenith at the Lahore Session of the All-India Muslim League in March 1940. Here, the famous Lahore Resolution, later known as the 'Pakistan Resolution,' was passed. This resolution called for the creation of 'independent states' for Muslims in the northwestern and eastern zones of India. This was a clear departure from his earlier stance and marked the formal demand for a separate Muslim state.

The Ideological Foundations of Pakistan
Jinnah's vision for Pakistan was rooted in several key ideas:

Religious Freedom and Protection: At the core of his demand was the protection of Muslim identity and religious practices in a land where they could exercise their rights without fear of domination by a Hindu majority.

Secular Governance: Despite advocating for a Muslim state, Jinnah envisioned Pakistan as a secular country. He famously stated in a speech on August 11, 1947, that in the state of Pakistan, religion or belief would have nothing to do with the business of the state.

Cultural and Economic Prosperity: Jinnah believed that Muslims could only achieve cultural and economic prosperity in a separate homeland where they were not overshadowed by a majority community.

Challenges and Criticisms
Jinnah's vision was not without its challenges and criticisms:

Feasibility and Implementation: Critics argued that the geographical and demographic complexity of the proposed Pakistan made its practical implementation difficult.

Concerns of Minority Communities: There were concerns about the fate of minority communities within the proposed Muslim state.
Political Opposition: The Congress and other political groups strongly opposed the idea, leading to intense political confrontations and negotiations.
Legacy and Impact:
The creation of Pakistan in 1947 stands as the most significant testament to Jinnah's vision. It altered the geopolitical landscape of South Asia and had profound implications for regional politics, communal relationships, and international relations. However, the partition that accompanied the birth of Pakistan led to massive communal violence and a massive population exchange, marking a tragic chapter in the subcontinent's history.
Conclusion:
Muhammad Ali Jinnah's evolving vision for a separate Muslim state underscores the complexity of political ideologies and their susceptibility to change under socio-political pressures. His journey from a unifier to a separatist reflects the tumultuous nature of the Indian independence movement and the intricate tapestry of communal relations in British India. Jinnah's legacy, marked by both admiration and controversy, continues to shape the discourse on nation-building, identity, and communal harmony in South Asia.

The ideological foundations of his demand for Pakistan

Muhammad Ali Jinnah, the founder of Pakistan, was a pivotal figure in South Asian history. His journey towards establishing Pakistan as a separate nation for Muslims in the Indian subcontinent was rooted in various ideological foundations. Understanding these foundations provides a deeper insight into Jinnah's vision and the creation of Pakistan.

Initial Political Stance
Initially, Jinnah was a firm believer in Hindu-Muslim unity in India. He joined the Indian National Congress (INC), the primary political party fighting for India's independence from British rule. His early political career was marked by efforts to bring Hindus and Muslims together to achieve this common goal.

Shift Towards Muslim Nationalism
However, over time, Jinnah grew disillusioned with the Congress, primarily due to what he perceived as its inability to properly represent Muslim interests. This disillusionment was a turning point, leading Jinnah to embrace the idea of a separate nation for Muslims.

Ideological Foundations of Pakistan
Two-Nation Theory: Central to Jinnah's demand for Pakistan was the Two-Nation Theory. He argued that Hindus and Muslims were not merely two religious groups but two distinct nations with different cultures, traditions, and social norms. This theory became the bedrock of his demand for a separate Muslim nation.

Fear of Minority Oppression: Jinnah was increasingly concerned about the future of Muslims as a minority in a predominantly Hindu India. He feared that Muslims would be politically, economically, and socially marginalized.

Preservation of Islamic Culture and Identity: Jinnah was keen on preserving the unique cultural and religious identity of Muslims. He believed that a separate nation would allow Muslims to practice their religion freely and maintain their cultural heritage.

Political and Economic Rights: Jinnah sought to secure political representation and economic opportunities for Muslims, which he felt could only be guaranteed in a separate Muslim state.

Lahore Resolution and Formal Demand for Pakistan
The Lahore Resolution of 1940, presented by the All-India Muslim League under Jinnah's leadership, formally demanded a separate nation for Muslims. This resolution marked a definitive shift in the Indian independence movement, setting the stage for the creation of Pakistan.

Jinnah's Vision for Pakistan
Jinnah envisioned Pakistan as a secular state with Muslims in the majority, rather than an Islamic theocracy. He wanted it to be a democratic nation where all citizens, regardless of religion, could enjoy equal rights. This vision was evident in his speech on August 11, 1947, where he outlined his hopes for religious freedom and equality in Pakistan.

Impact and Legacy

Jinnah's relentless advocacy for Pakistan bore fruit on August 14, 1947, when Pakistan was established as a separate nation. His ideological stance had a profound impact on the subcontinent's history and continues to influence the political and social fabric of Pakistan.

Jinnah's journey from a proponent of Hindu-Muslim unity to the architect of a separate Muslim nation illustrates the complexities of colonial India's political landscape. His transformation was not abrupt but evolved through a series of political experiences and observations.

Conclusion

Muhammad Ali Jinnah's demand for Pakistan was rooted in a deep concern for the rights and identity of Muslims in a post-colonial Indian subcontinent. His vision was shaped by his experiences, observations, and political interactions. The ideological foundations laid by Jinnah continue to influence the discourse on national identity, religious freedom, and minority rights in South Asia. His legacy, encapsulated in the creation of Pakistan, stands as a testament to his political acumen and his unwavering commitment to his beliefs.

Jinnah's story is not just about the creation of a nation but also about the enduring power of ideology and vision in shaping the course of history. His life and actions offer valuable lessons in leadership, resilience, and the pursuit of one's convictions, making him a pivotal figure in the annals of modern history.

Chapter 6: The All-India Muslim League

Leadership of the All-India Muslim League

Muhammad Ali Jinnah, a figure of pivotal importance in the history of the Indian subcontinent, emerged as a distinctive leader who played a crucial role in the creation of Pakistan. His journey as a political figure and his leadership within the All-India Muslim League were marked by a series of significant events and shifts in his political ideology.

Early Political Career and Joining the Muslim League: Jinnah began his political journey as a member of the Indian National Congress, advocating for Hindu-Muslim unity. His initial stance was characterized by efforts to bridge communal divides, exemplified by his involvement in the 1916 Lucknow Pact, a significant agreement between the Congress and the Muslim League which he helped shape. This period was marked by his advocacy for constitutional reforms to safeguard the political rights of Muslims within a united Indian subcontinent.

Shift in Political Views and the Lahore Resolution: By the 1940s, Jinnah's perspective had shifted considerably. He began to advocate for a separate nation for Muslims, driven by concerns over their marginalization in a predominantly Hindu India. This culminated in the 1940 Lahore Resolution, where the Muslim League, under Jinnah's leadership, demanded a separate nation for Indian Muslims. This marked a significant departure from his earlier stance of Hindu-Muslim unity and laid the groundwork for the eventual creation of Pakistan.

Jinnah's Leadership Style:
Jinnah was known for his eloquence, legal acumen, and political tact. His leadership style was characterized by a blend of firmness and diplomatic finesse. He was admired internationally for his political skill, often drawing comparisons with notable figures in terms of his speech and demeanor. His transformation from a champion of Hindu-Muslim unity to the principal advocate for a separate Muslim nation illustrates his adaptability and strategic thinking in the face of changing political landscapes.

The Creation of Pakistan and Partition:
The period leading up to the partition of India was marked by intense negotiations and political maneuvering. Jinnah, as the leader of the Muslim League, played a critical role in these events. The demand for Pakistan was rooted in the belief that Muslims in India would be politically and socially marginalized in a Hindu-majority independent India. This led to the eventual creation of Pakistan in 1947, a momentous event that Jinnah had tirelessly worked towards. However, this period was also marred by communal violence and mass migrations, as the subcontinent was divided along religious lines.

Legacy and Impact:
Jinnah's political journey from an advocate of Hindu-Muslim unity to the founder of a separate Muslim nation remains a subject of considerable study and debate. His impact on the history of the Indian subcontinent is undeniable. He is revered in Pakistan as

the father of the nation, while his role and actions continue to be analyzed and interpreted in various ways across the region.

Jinnah's leadership of the All-India Muslim League thus represents a complex tapestry of political change, marked by his evolving views on communal harmony and national identity. His contributions, both in the creation of Pakistan and in shaping the political discourse of his time, continue to resonate in the history of South Asia.

Support for the demand for Pakistan

 Muhammad Ali Jinnah, a towering figure in the history of South Asia, played an instrumental role in the creation of Pakistan. His journey from a barrister to the founder of a nation is a testament to his unwavering commitment and strategic political acumen.

Jinnah's strategic efforts in mobilizing support for the creation of Pakistan were multifaceted. In 1934, he returned to politics in India and quickly ascended the ranks to become the leader of the Muslim League. His political maneuvering during this period was crucial. For instance, he used the 1935 Government of India Act to regain influence and strategically allied with regional leaders to strengthen the Muslim League's position. The 1937 elections, despite initial setbacks, turned to his advantage as he capitalized on the Congress Party's mistakes, positioning the Muslim League as the sole protector of Muslim interests.

The Lahore Resolution of 1940, which Jinnah played a significant role in drafting, called for the creation of independent states for Muslims in the northwestern and eastern regions of India. This resolution marked a pivotal turn in his strategy, as it laid the groundwork for the eventual creation of Pakistan. Jinnah's negotiation skills were key during this period, especially in dealings with the British government and the Indian National Congress. His unwavering commitment to Muslim rights and leadership during these tumultuous times were central to the establishment of Pakistan.

As Pakistan's first Governor-General, Jinnah faced immense challenges. The partition of India led to a massive refugee crisis and communal violence. Despite his deteriorating health, Jinnah worked tirelessly to stabilize the nation and lay the foundations for a democratic and modern state. His advocacy for minority rights and his vision of Pakistan as a progressive and inclusive nation were evident in his policy priorities. He emphasized education, industrialization, and economic development as pillars for a prosperous nation.

Jinnah's leadership style was characterized by determination, intellect, and integrity. His ability to communicate effectively and inspire people was pivotal in the struggle for Pakistan. His speeches and addresses played a significant role in mobilizing public support for the creation of Pakistan. Sadly, Jinnah passed away on September 11, 1948, leaving a profound void in the leadership of the newly-formed nation.

In conclusion, Muhammad Ali Jinnah's role in the creation of Pakistan was monumental. His strategic leadership, skilled negotiations, and vision shaped the destiny of a nation. His legacy continues to inspire generations in Pakistan, where he is remembered as the Father of the Nation and a symbol of unity and national pride.

Challenges in his pursuit of a separate Muslim homeland

Muhammad Ali Jinnah, the founder and first governor-general of Pakistan, faced numerous challenges in his pursuit of a separate Muslim homeland. His political journey was marked by a complex interplay of ideological shifts, strategic decisions, and the struggle to balance diverse interests within a politically charged environment of British India.

Early Political Involvement and Shift in Perspective
Jinnah started his political career with the Indian National Congress (INC), initially aligning with its moderate faction and advocating for Hindu-Muslim unity. His stance at this time earned him the reputation of being an "ambassador of Hindu-Muslim unity" (Britannica). However, Jinnah's perspective began to shift due to several factors. He was disillusioned with the INC's approach towards minority rights, particularly concerning Muslims, and disagreed with Gandhi's method of non-cooperation, which he believed could lead to lawlessness (IAS Express). These ideological differences eventually led him to distance himself from the INC and align more closely with the All India Muslim League.

Challenges in Safeguarding Muslim Interests
Jinnah's transition to the Muslim League marked a significant turn in his political ideology. He became increasingly concerned about the political marginalization of Muslims in a Hindu-majority India. The demographic composition of India and the vast differences between Hindu and Muslim cultures, traditions, and religious practices intensified these

concerns (IAS Express). Jinnah realized that constitutional reforms within the British system might not adequately safeguard Muslim interests and identity.

Strategic Maneuvering and the Lahore Resolution
Jinnah's political acumen was evident in his strategic maneuvers. He skillfully navigated the complex political landscape, balancing the demands of different Muslim factions and the broader Indian nationalist movement. The Lahore Resolution of 1940, which proposed the idea of a separate nation for Muslims, was a pivotal moment in this regard. Jinnah played a central role in this resolution, emphasizing the distinct cultural and political identity of Muslims (IAS Express). This resolution laid the groundwork for the eventual creation of Pakistan.

External Influences and Support
Jinnah's vision was also influenced and supported by other key figures. Figures like Sir Sultan Muhammad Shah, the Aga Khan, played a significant role in promoting Muslim interests both in India and England (Hilal English). Allama Muhammad Iqbal, a prominent philosopher and poet, also played a crucial role. He believed that Indian Muslims constituted a 'political nationality' and advocated for a separate homeland for Muslims. Iqbal's ideas and support were instrumental in encouraging Jinnah to take up the leadership of the Muslim League and pursue the creation of Pakistan (Hilal English).

Legacy and Post-Independence Challenges
Jinnah's vision and efforts culminated in the creation of Pakistan in 1947. However, the journey did not end there. The nascent nation faced numerous struggles in achieving and maintaining independent nation-

statehood. Issues like national security, sovereignty, provincial, linguistic, and ethnic tensions continued to shape Pakistan's trajectory post-independence. Jinnah's legacy, while monumental, also became a subject of debate as successive leaders interpreted and reinterpreted his vision to suit their political agendas (Project MUSE).

In summary, Muhammad Ali Jinnah's quest for a separate Muslim homeland was fraught with challenges, both internal and external. His political journey from a proponent of Hindu-Muslim unity to the champion of a separate Muslim nation underscores the complexities of the political and social milieu of British India. His strategic vision, political agility, and unwavering commitment to Muslim interests played a crucial role in the creation of Pakistan, but the challenges did not cease with its formation. The legacy and interpretation of Jinnah's vision continued to influence the political and social fabric of Pakistan long after its independence.

Obstacles faced by Jinnah

Muhammad Ali Jinnah, known as the founder of Pakistan, faced a myriad of obstacles in his quest to establish a separate Muslim homeland. His journey was characterized by political, societal, and personal challenges, each intertwining to form a complex tapestry of struggle and perseverance.

Early Political Challenges
Jinnah's political journey began as a member of the Indian National Congress, where he initially worked for Hindu-Muslim unity. However, he soon realized the depth of communal divisions and the need for a separate Muslim identity in politics. This realization marked the genesis of his transformation from an Indian nationalist to the leader of the All-India Muslim League.

1. Challenge of Representation:
Context: In the early 20th century, Muslims in India were politically underrepresented and socio-economically marginalized.
Jinnah's Response: He advocated for the rights of Muslims within the broader Indian political framework, initially striving for unity but gradually moving towards separatism.
2. Congress-League Rift:
Context: The rift between the Indian National Congress and the Muslim League became pronounced, especially after the Nehru Report (1928), which Jinnah found unsatisfactory for safeguarding Muslim interests.
Jinnah's Response: He formulated the Fourteen Points in 1929, which became the cornerstone of Muslim demands and reflected his commitment to protecting Muslim identity and rights.

Societal and Ideological Challenges
Jinnah's idea of a separate Muslim homeland was not
only a political movement but also a societal and
ideological struggle.

3. Communal Tensions:
Context: India witnessed escalating communal tensions,
culminating in events like the Direct Action Day in
1946.
Jinnah's Response: Despite being a secularist in
personal life, Jinnah used Islamic symbolism and
rhetoric to galvanize Muslim support, while
simultaneously advocating for a homeland where
Muslims could thrive without fear of domination.
4. Differing Visions Within Muslim Leadership:
Context: Not all Muslim leaders or the populace were
initially in favor of partition; many envisioned a united
India with protected Muslim rights.
Jinnah's Response: Through persuasive speeches and
political maneuvering, Jinnah gradually convinced a
significant portion of the Muslim population of the
necessity of a separate nation.
Personal Challenges
Jinnah's personal life was not devoid of challenges,
which often intersected with his political pursuits.

5. Health Issues:
Context: Jinnah's health started deteriorating in the
1940s, even as he was deeply involved in intense
political negotiations.
Jinnah's Response: Despite severe illness, he continued
to lead the Muslim League, showcasing remarkable
resilience.

6. Balancing Secularism and Religious Identity:
Context: As a secular Muslim, Jinnah's personal beliefs sometimes clashed with the increasing religiosity of the movement he led.
Jinnah's Response: He maintained a delicate balance, advocating for a state where Islam was a cultural and moral guide but not the basis of government.
Strategic and Diplomatic Challenges
Jinnah's strategy had to evolve constantly to cope with the rapidly changing political landscape of pre-independent India.

7. Negotiations with the British and Congress:
Context: The British government's stance and the Congress Party's opposition were significant hurdles.
Jinnah's Response: He engaged in complex negotiations, using legal acumen and political savvy to advance the cause of Pakistan.
8. Partition Violence:
Context: The partition of India led to unprecedented communal violence.
Jinnah's Response: He condemned the violence and worked towards establishing peace and order in the newly formed Pakistan, though the scale of the tragedy was overwhelming.
Conclusion
Jinnah's journey in creating Pakistan was a blend of resilience, strategic diplomacy, and an unyielding commitment to a vision that was fraught with challenges at every step. His legacy is a testament to the power of determination in the face of seemingly insurmountable obstacles.

Chapter 7: Lahore Resolution and the Pakistan Movement

Popular support for the idea of Pakistan

Muhammad Ali Jinnah, a figure synonymous with the creation and shaping of Pakistan, stands as a towering personality in the annals of South Asian history. His journey, marked by intellectual rigor, political acumen, and an unyielding commitment to his cause, culminates in his pivotal role during the Lahore Resolution and the subsequent Pakistan Movement. This narrative will delve into the intricacies of his life and his indispensable role in the founding of Pakistan, elucidating aspects often overshadowed in mainstream history.

Initial Political Forays
Initially, Jinnah was a member of the Indian National Congress, passionately advocating for Hindu-Muslim unity. His eloquence and legal expertise rapidly elevated his stature, yet the political landscape of India, rife with communal tensions, gradually steered his path towards a more focused advocacy for Muslim rights.

The Turning Point: Lahore Resolution
The Lahore Resolution in March 1940, which Jinnah orchestrated, was a defining moment in South Asian history. It was here that the idea of a separate nation for Muslims was articulated unambiguously for the first time. Jinnah's speech at this event was a masterclass in oratory and political strategy. He meticulously outlined the need for a separate Muslim homeland, citing

historical, cultural, and economic reasons, while emphasizing the growing rifts between Hindus and Muslims.

The Pakistan Movement: A Test of Resilience and Diplomacy
Post-Lahore Resolution, Jinnah's role in the Pakistan Movement was multifaceted. He became the linchpin in mobilizing Muslim sentiment across India. His ability to navigate the complex political terrain, marked by British colonial interests and Hindu-majority nationalism, was remarkable. He employed a blend of legal expertise, political negotiation, and mass mobilization to further his cause.

Key Strategies
Diplomatic Engagement: Jinnah adeptly engaged with British authorities, presenting the case for Pakistan as a logical outcome of the British policy of divide and rule.
Mass Mobilization: Utilizing his oratory skills, Jinnah galvanized Muslim masses, transforming the Pakistan Movement into a popular struggle.
Legal Frameworks: His legal acumen was pivotal in formulating the arguments for Pakistan's feasibility and necessity.
The Partition and Birth of Pakistan
August 14, 1947, marked the culmination of Jinnah's relentless struggle, with the creation of Pakistan.
Jinnah's leadership during the partition was a testament to his stoicism amid chaos. He faced monumental challenges: massive population transfers, communal riots, and the establishment of a new government's structure.

Legacy and Controversies
Jinnah's legacy is complex. Revered in Pakistan as the 'Quaid-e-Azam' (Great Leader), his vision for Pakistan is often debated. He envisioned a secular Pakistan where religion would not be the business of the state, a vision that seems to diverge from the course Pakistan eventually took.

Conclusion
In retrospect, Jinnah's role in the Lahore Resolution and the Pakistan Movement was not just about the creation of a new nation. It was a demonstration of political sagacity, resilience in the face of overwhelming odds, and a testament to his belief in the right of self-determination. His life, marked by a journey from a nationalist to the founder of a nation, remains an enduring study in leadership, diplomacy, and the complexities of human aspirations.

Challenges of uniting diverse Muslim communities

Muhammad Ali Jinnah, revered as the founder of Pakistan, faced a myriad of intricate challenges in uniting the diverse Muslim communities of India behind his vision for a separate homeland. This journey was riddled with a complex interplay of religious, cultural, political, and linguistic elements, requiring a deft balancing act that Jinnah managed with remarkable acumen.

1. Religious Diversity Within Muslim Communities
Jinnah's vision of a Muslim homeland was not just a political movement; it was deeply rooted in the religious diversity that existed within the Muslim communities of India. These communities, ranging from Sunni and Shia Muslims to smaller sects like the Ahmadiyyas and Sufis, had varied interpretations of Islam. Jinnah, who was known for his secular approach, had to carefully navigate these religious differences, emphasizing the commonalities and downplaying the internal religious conflicts. His task was to present the idea of Pakistan as a unifying goal, transcending sectarian divides.

2. Cultural and Linguistic Diversity
The Muslim population in India was not a monolith but a tapestry of diverse cultures and languages. From the Urdu-speaking Muslims in the United Provinces to the Bengali-speaking populace in East Bengal, and from the Punjabis in the north to the Sindhis and Balochis in the west, each group had its unique cultural identity. Jinnah had to unify these culturally distinct groups under the singular banner of Muslim nationalism, often

employing Urdu as the lingua franca to foster a sense of unity.

3. Political Disparities and Leadership Conflicts
Jinnah faced significant challenges in aligning various Muslim political factions towards the idea of Pakistan. He contended with regional leaderships, like those in Bengal and Punjab, who had their vested interests and were often skeptical of a centralized authority that Pakistan represented. Jinnah's political dexterity was evident in how he negotiated with these regional powerhouses, assuaging their fears while keeping the larger goal in focus.

4. Economic Concerns of Muslim Landlords and Businessmen
Many Muslim landlords and businessmen were apprehensive about the economic implications of a separate Muslim state. Their fortunes were deeply intertwined with the economic framework of united India. Jinnah had to assure these influential groups that their economic interests would be safeguarded in Pakistan. His assurances were crucial in swaying the economically powerful segments of Muslim society.

5. Dealing with British Colonial Authorities
Negotiating with the British rulers was a significant challenge. Jinnah had to demonstrate that the demand for Pakistan was a democratic aspiration of the Muslim majority areas and not just a political maneuver. His legal background and his reputation as an upright leader helped him in these negotiations, where he presented the case for Pakistan with astuteness and fervor.

6. Opposition from Indian National Congress
The most formidable challenge was perhaps the opposition from the Indian National Congress. Leaders like Gandhi and Nehru were vehemently against the idea of partition based on religious lines. Jinnah had to counter their arguments, both in public forums and in negotiations, stressing that the Muslims of India needed a separate nation to safeguard their rights and identity.

7. Internal Debates over the Concept of Pakistan
Within the Muslim League and its supporters, there were debates about the nature of Pakistan. While some envisioned it as a modern, secular state with Islam as a cultural component, others saw it as an Islamic state governed by Sharia law. Jinnah had to balance these internal views, crafting a vision of Pakistan that was broad enough to encompass various perspectives.

8. Addressing the Fears of Minority Communities
Another challenge was addressing the fears of non-Muslim minority communities within the proposed areas of Pakistan. Hindus, Sikhs, and Christians were apprehensive about their future in a Muslim-majority state. Jinnah had to reassure these communities that their rights would be protected, attempting to foster a vision of an inclusive Pakistan.

9. Geographical and Administrative Challenges
The geographical layout of Muslim-majority areas presented another challenge. These areas were not contiguous but scattered, with significant distances between West and East Pakistan. Jinnah had to envision an administrative structure that could efficiently govern such a geographically fragmented nation.

10. Personal Health Issues
Amidst all these challenges, Jinnah's personal health
was deteriorating. His unwavering dedication to his
cause often came at the cost of his health. Despite his
physical frailty, he continued to lead the movement
with indomitable spirit, symbolizing the resilience and
determination that the creation of Pakistan required.

Muhammad Ali Jinnah's journey in uniting the diverse
Muslim communities of India under the singular goal of
creating Pakistan stands as a testament to his political
sagacity, his unyielding commitment to his vision, and
his ability to transcend the myriad divides that
fragmented the subcontinent's Muslim populace.

Chapter 8: Negotiations with the British and Congress

Jinnah's negotiations with the British government

Muhammad Ali Jinnah, remembered as the architect of Pakistan, undertook a complex and nuanced journey in his negotiations with the British government, which ultimately led to the creation of Pakistan. His early political career, strategic negotiations, and the eventual realization of his vision offer a rich tapestry of historical events that shaped the subcontinent's destiny.

Early Political Involvement and Ideological Shift

Initially a member of the Indian National Congress, Jinnah was a strong proponent of Hindu-Muslim unity and sought constitutional reforms within the British Empire. His political ideology evolved over time, especially after the 1916 Lucknow Pact, which he played a key role in shaping. The pact was a moment of Hindu-Muslim unity, but its ineffective implementation led Jinnah to gradually advocate for the distinct political rights of Muslims in India.

Lahore Resolution and the Concept of Pakistan

The year 1940 was a turning point when the Muslim League, under Jinnah's leadership, passed the Lahore Resolution, demanding a separate nation for Muslims. This bold move was a departure from earlier calls for constitutional safeguards for Muslims within a united

India and directly challenged the British policy of maintaining a unified Indian state.

Strategic Engagements with the British

Jinnah's negotiations with the British were marked by his legal expertise, political savvy, and an unwavering commitment to his cause. He astutely navigated the political landscape, balancing constitutional arguments with political realities.

Cripps Mission (1942): Jinnah's refusal of the Cripps proposal was based on his insistence on the integrity of Muslim-majority areas in any future division.

Simla Conference (1945): Jinnah's demand to be recognized as the sole representative of Indian Muslims significantly elevated the Muslim League's political stature.

Cabinet Mission Plan (1946): Initially accepting the plan for a federated India with autonomous provinces, Jinnah later rejected it due to its inconsistent interpretation by the Congress, highlighting his commitment to a clear vision for Pakistan.

Direct Action Day (1946): This was a strategic move to showcase the strength of Muslim League and the urgency of the Muslim demand for a separate nation.

Mountbatten Plan (1947): Jinnah's acceptance of this plan, which called for a partition and a swift British exit, was a pragmatic step, realizing that it offered the most feasible path to a separate Muslim state.

Jinnah's Lasting Legacy in Negotiations

Jinnah's approach to negotiations with the British was a blend of legal acumen, political strategy, and adaptability. His actions and decisions were instrumental in shaping the future of the Indian subcontinent. However, the rapid execution of the partition plan and unresolved issues led to significant challenges for the newly formed nation, including communal violence and administrative difficulties.

In sum, Jinnah's negotiations with the British government were a testament to his political foresight, legal expertise, and strategic maneuvering. His legacy in this regard is a complex interplay of achievements and challenges, emblematic of the tumultuous path to the creation of Pakistan.

Indian National Congress in the lead-up

Muhammad Ali Jinnah's journey through Indian politics, particularly his role in the Indian National Congress (INC) and his transition to the leader of the All-India Muslim League, is a story of ideological evolution and the complexities of pre-partition politics in British India.

Jinnah's early political career was characterized by his advocacy for Hindu–Muslim unity. He rose to prominence within the INC in the first two decades of the 20th century. During this time, he played a significant role in shaping the 1916 Lucknow Pact between the Congress and the All-India Muslim League, a key moment demonstrating his dedication to the cause of Hindu-Muslim unity.

In the political landscape of the time, Jinnah was recognized as a leading figure advocating for a united, free India, where the interests and rights of the Muslim community would be acknowledged and protected. His efforts were in line with the aspirations expressed by others, such as Iqbal, emphasizing cooperation between communities for the progress of India.

However, the trajectory of Indian politics and Jinnah's personal beliefs began to change. The advent of Gandhi's leadership brought a new dimension to the Indian freedom struggle, characterized by mass movements like civil disobedience and non-cooperation. Gandhi's approach differed significantly from Jinnah's belief in constitutional reform and political negotiation. Jinnah's disillusionment with the

INC's approach, particularly regarding minority rights and the method of non-cooperation advocated by Gandhi, led to his resignation from the Congress in 1920.

Post-resignation, Jinnah's focus shifted towards exclusively representing Muslim interests. His efforts in the Muslim League were driven by a growing concern about the political and cultural future of Muslims in an independent India. This culminated in his support for the Two-Nation Theory and the demand for a separate nation for Indian Muslims, which he articulated in the 1940 Lahore Resolution. Jinnah's transformation from an ambassador of Hindu-Muslim unity to the proponent of a separate Muslim state is reflective of the turbulent and divisive politics of the era.

Jinnah's leadership in the Muslim League and his pivotal role in advocating for Pakistan's creation showcased his enduring impact on the Indian subcontinent's history. His actions and decisions during this period were instrumental in shaping the course of South Asian history, leading to the partition of India in 1947 and the emergence of Pakistan as a separate nation.

Jinnah's political journey is a testament to the dynamic and often contentious nature of the struggle for independence in British India. His legacy continues to be a subject of study and reflection in the context of the region's history and the complex interplay of religious, cultural, and political factors that shaped the era.

Complex political dynamics for partition of Indian subcontinent

Analyzing the complex political dynamics that led to the partition of the Indian subcontinent is a multifaceted and intricate task. This significant historical event was the culmination of a series of political, social, religious, and economic factors, each contributing to the eventual division of India into two separate nations: India and Pakistan. The heart of this division can be attributed to several key elements, each intertwined with the other, creating a tapestry of events that led to the creation of Pakistan in 1947.

1. Historical Context and Colonial Legacy
The British Raj, which governed India from 1858 to 1947, played a pivotal role in shaping the political landscape of the subcontinent. British policies of divide and rule, economic exploitation, and administrative decisions laid the groundwork for communal tensions. The partition was not just a political separation but also a result of deep-rooted historical grievances and differences exacerbated by colonial rule.

2. The Rise of Nationalism
The early 20th century saw the rise of Indian nationalism, a movement that sought to end British rule. However, this nationalism was not a monolith; it comprised various factions and ideologies. The Indian National Congress, primarily representing Hindu interests, and the All-India Muslim League, representing Muslim interests, became the two dominant political entities. Their differing visions for a post-colonial India sowed the seeds of partition.

3. The Communal Divide

The religious divide between Hindus and Muslims played a critical role in the partition. This divide was not merely religious but also had socio-economic and cultural dimensions. Muslims feared marginalization in a Hindu-majority India. This fear was manipulated by political leaders on both sides, leading to communal riots and deepening mistrust.

4. The Role of Key Leaders

Leaders like Mohandas Karamchand Gandhi, Jawaharlal Nehru, and Muhammad Ali Jinnah were central figures in this period. Gandhi's vision of a united India clashed with Jinnah's demand for a separate Muslim state. The contrasting ideologies of these leaders significantly influenced the political discourse and decision-making process.

5. The Lahore Resolution and the Demand for Pakistan

The Lahore Resolution of 1940, passed by the Muslim League, formally demanded a separate nation for Muslims. This resolution marked a definitive shift from seeking Muslim rights within a united India to demanding a separate nation – Pakistan.

6. The Impact of World War II

World War II weakened the British Empire, hastening the end of colonial rule. The war's aftermath saw Britain's reduced capacity to manage its empire, including India. The urgency to transfer power was intensified by the war's economic and political repercussions.

7. The Direct Action Day and Communal Violence

The announcement of Direct-Action Day in 1946 by the Muslim League led to unprecedented communal violence, highlighting the extent of religious polarization. This violence demonstrated the impracticality of a united India and pushed leaders towards accepting partition as a solution.

8. The British Role in Partition

The British, particularly Lord Mountbatten, the last Viceroy of India, played a significant role in the final decision to partition. The haste with which the British executed the partition plan, with little consideration for the practical implications, led to chaos, violence, and a massive refugee crisis.

9. The Socio-Economic Factors

Socio-economic factors, such as the disparity in education and employment opportunities between Hindus and Muslims, contributed to the widening divide. The economic policies of the British Raj often favored certain communities, creating resentment and fear of domination post-independence.

10. The Boundary Commission and Radcliffe Line

The Boundary Commission, led by Sir Cyril Radcliffe, was tasked with drawing the borders between India and Pakistan. The Radcliffe Line, drawn hastily and without comprehensive understanding of the local dynamics, led to further violence and displacement.

Conclusion:

The partition of the Indian subcontinent was a complex phenomenon influenced by a multitude of factors. It was not just a political event but also a tragic human saga, marked by mass migrations, violence, and the uprooting of communities. Understanding the dynamics of partition requires a nuanced appreciation of the historical, social, and political intricacies of that era. The creation of Pakistan was not merely the birth of a new nation but the culmination of a struggle defined by a complex interplay of diverse and often conflicting political, religious, and cultural forces.

Competing interests that influenced the negotiations

The partition of the Indian subcontinent in 1947, which led to the creation of India and Pakistan, was a culmination of a series of complex negotiations shaped by various competing interests. These interests ranged from political ideologies and religious identities to colonial strategies and personal ambitions. Here, we will explore these diverse influences that steered the course of these historical negotiations.

1. Colonial Interests of the British Empire
The British Empire, ruling India since the mid-18th century, had its own set of priorities. Post World War II, Britain was economically weakened and sought a swift exit from India, but with minimal disruption to its geopolitical interests. The British were also keen to ensure that the newly independent dominions remained within the Commonwealth and were allies in the Cold War context.

2. Congress and Its Vision of a Secular India
The Indian National Congress, led by figures like Jawaharlal Nehru and Mahatma Gandhi, advocated for a secular India where Hindus and Muslims could coexist. They envisioned a single nation, devoid of religious divisions, grounded in democratic principles. Their resistance to partition was rooted in this ideal of a united, diverse India.

3. Muslim League's Demand for a Separate Nation
Under the leadership of Muhammad Ali Jinnah, the All-India Muslim League argued that Muslims in India would be politically and socially marginalized in a

Hindu-majority India. They pushed for the creation of Pakistan, a separate nation for Muslims, as a safeguard against potential oppression and to preserve Islamic cultural and religious identity.

4. Religious and Communal Tensions

The late 1940s witnessed heightened communal tensions between Hindus and Muslims. These tensions were partly stoked by political rhetoric and partly by historical grievances. The fear of being dominated by the other community became a powerful force driving the call for separate homelands.

5. Regional Princes and Their Ambitions

India was not just British India; it also comprised numerous princely states. These states, ruled by local monarchs, were diverse in size and allegiance. Many of these princes desired to maintain their autonomy post-independence, influencing the negotiation dynamics.

6. International Geopolitical Dynamics

The global context of the Cold War era also played a role. The strategic location of the Indian subcontinent made its political orientation significant to both the USA and the USSR. Additionally, the presence of Afghanistan and the Middle East nearby added to the geopolitical complexity.

7. Economic Considerations and Divisions

Economic factors such as resource allocation, division of assets, and management of debts also influenced the negotiations. Both sides wanted to ensure they received a fair share of resources, including financial reserves and military assets.

8. Personal Ambitions and Rivalries
Personal ambitions and rivalries among the leading figures of the Congress and the Muslim League also impacted the course of the negotiations. The personal dynamics between leaders like Jinnah, Nehru, and Gandhi shaped the nature and outcome of the discussions.

9. Socio-Cultural Factors
Socio-cultural factors, including language, culture, and historical narratives, played a role. Different regions had their own unique identities and histories, which influenced their stance on the partition.

10. The Influence of Grassroots Movements
Lastly, grassroots movements and public opinion cannot be overlooked. The sentiments of the ordinary people, often fueled by local incidents and propaganda, influenced the high-level political negotiations.

In conclusion, the partition of the Indian subcontinent was not merely a decision made in conference rooms; it was a complex, multifaceted process influenced by a myriad of competing interests. From the imperial strategies of the British to the religious and cultural aspirations of the subcontinent's diverse populace, every factor contributed to the shaping of this monumental event in South Asian history. Each interest, with its unique perspective and goal, wove together to create a tapestry of negotiations that ultimately led to the creation of two independent nations, India and Pakistan.

Chapter 9: Partition and Independence

Detailed exploration of the partition of India

The Partition of India in 1947 stands as one of the most pivotal and traumatic events in the history of South Asia. This monumental incident not only led to the creation of two independent dominions, India and Pakistan, but it also unleashed a scale of communal violence and mass migrations seldom seen in history. In this extensive exploration, we delve into the various facets of this historical event, encompassing its roots, the complex process, its immediate aftermath, and its lasting impact on the region and beyond.

Historical Background
The seeds of partition were sown much before 1947. The British Raj, ruling over the Indian subcontinent since the mid-19th century, implemented policies that often played on the religious divide between Hindus and Muslims. The formation of the All India Muslim League in 1906 and the Indian National Congress's earlier establishment in 1885 created platforms for political expression but also highlighted communal divisions. The concept of a separate Muslim state was first articulated by Allama Iqbal in 1930, and it gained momentum with Muhammad Ali Jinnah's leadership of the Muslim League.

The Path to Partition
The decisive phase began with the end of World War II in 1945. The Labour government in Britain, under

Clement Attlee, was keen on transferring power swiftly in India but was confronted with the complex challenge of accommodating the conflicting aspirations of the Congress and the Muslim League. The Cabinet Mission Plan of 1946, which proposed a federal structure with a weak center, was unable to prevent the drift towards partition.

The Mountbatten Plan and Its Execution
Lord Mountbatten, the last Viceroy of India, proposed a plan in June 1947, which expedited the process of partition. It called for the division of British India into India and Pakistan, with Punjab and Bengal also being split between the two new countries. The haste with which this plan was implemented, with the boundary commission led by Sir Cyril Radcliffe, had profound implications. Radcliffe, with limited knowledge of Indian conditions and under immense time pressure, drew boundaries that were to be a source of contention for years to come.

The Human Tragedy
The immediate aftermath of partition was catastrophic. The drawing of borders led to massive population movements - over 15 million people were estimated to have been displaced. Hindus and Sikhs from what was now Pakistan moved to India, and Muslims in India moved to Pakistan. This migration was accompanied by horrific communal violence, with estimates of casualties ranging from several hundred thousand to two million. The violence, loss, and trauma of this period left deep scars and continue to affect Indo-Pak relations to this day.

Socio-Political Aftermath and Legacy

The impact of partition extended beyond the immediate violence. It had far-reaching socio-political implications. It altered demographic compositions, leading to significant minority populations in both countries. The Kashmir dispute, a direct outcome of partition, remains one of the most enduring and dangerous conflicts in the region. Partition also had a profound impact on cultural and social structures, affecting literature, art, and cinema, often reflecting the pain and nostalgia of those uprooted.

Conclusion

The partition of India was not just a geopolitical event but a deeply personal tragedy for millions. It reshaped the subcontinent's political landscape and continues to influence the socio-political dynamics between India and Pakistan. Understanding the complexities and human dimensions of this event is crucial for grasping the contemporary challenges and aspirations of South Asia.

This exploration into the partition of India reveals the multifaceted nature of historical events, where political decisions have far-reaching and often unforeseen human consequences. The partition serves as a poignant reminder of the impact of colonialism, the power of nationalist movements, and the enduring legacy of decisions made in moments of crisis.

The emergence of Pakistan as an independent nation

The emergence of Pakistan as an independent nation is a tale steeped in a complex web of historical, cultural, and political intricacies. It's a saga marked by the confluence of myriad forces - colonialism, nationalism, and the relentless struggle for identity and self-determination. This narrative unfolds over several decades, culminating in the creation of a new nation on August 14, 1947.

The Colonial Context
The subcontinent's journey towards independence began under the shadow of British colonial rule. The British Raj, as it was known, had established a stronghold in the region by the mid-19th century, fundamentally altering the political and social fabric of the land. It was within this context that the seeds of an independent Pakistan were sown.

The Ideological Genesis
The idea of Pakistan, initially, was more ideological than geographical. It was envisioned by thinkers like Allama Iqbal, who, in his presidential address to the Muslim League in 1930, articulated the need for a separate Muslim state. This idea stemmed from the fear of marginalization of Muslims in a Hindu-majority independent India. Iqbal's vision was grounded in the desire for a space where Muslims could practice their cultural and religious traditions freely.

The Political Mobilization
The torchbearer of this vision was Muhammad Ali Jinnah, a barrister and politician, who emerged as the

leader of the All-India Muslim League. Jinnah initially worked for Hindu-Muslim unity but later became convinced that Muslims in India would not receive fair political representation in an independent India dominated by the Hindu majority. His persuasive oratory and unwavering commitment to the cause of a separate nation for Muslims galvanized a significant portion of the Muslim population.

The Lahore Resolution
A pivotal moment in this journey was the Lahore Resolution in 1940, where the Muslim League formally demanded a separate nation for Muslims. This resolution marked a definitive shift from seeking minority safeguards within a united India to demanding an entirely separate state.

The Partition and Its Aftermath
The culmination of these efforts, negotiations, and struggles was the partition of British India into two independent dominions: India and Pakistan. This partition, however, was not without its profound and traumatic consequences. The drawing of borders by the British led to one of the largest mass migrations in human history, accompanied by communal violence and upheaval that left deep scars on both sides.

The Birth of Pakistan
On August 14, 1947, Pakistan emerged on the world map, consisting of two geographically and culturally distinct regions, West Pakistan (modern-day Pakistan) and East Pakistan (now Bangladesh). Jinnah became the new nation's first Governor-General, and Liaquat Ali Khan its first Prime Minister. The joy of independence was, however, tempered by the immense challenges the

young nation faced - from setting up a new government to handling the influx of millions of refugees.

The Legacy

The emergence of Pakistan as an independent nation is a testament to the power of a shared vision, relentless struggle, and the complex interplay of historical forces. It serves as a poignant reminder of the quest for identity and self-determination, echoing the aspirations and turmoil that characterize the birth of nations.

Conclusion

Pakistan's birth was not just the creation of a new political entity; it was the culmination of a profound and transformative journey that reshaped the Indian subcontinent. It stands as a significant chapter in the annals of colonial history and the worldwide struggle for self-governance and cultural identity. The story of Pakistan's emergence is a vivid tapestry, woven with the threads of aspiration, conflict, and the indomitable human spirit.

Jinnah's leadership during this tumultuous period

Muhammad Ali Jinnah's leadership in the period
following the partition of India was marked by his
unique approach to handling the complex Hindu-
Muslim question and his advocacy for the Muslim
cause. His leadership style was significantly influenced
by British liberal traditions and his legal profession,
which provided him with the necessary tools to
critically examine British rule and its impact on
Muslims in India.

Jinnah was acutely aware of the new political landscape
that Muslims faced in India due to the British
establishment of a legal-rational state authority,
professional bureaucracy, representative institutions,
and a new court system. He recognized that Muslims
needed to be effectively represented in these institutions
to avoid being marginalized. Jinnah's efforts were
focused on protecting and advancing the Muslim
political identity, rights, and interests within the
framework of the modern state system. Unlike many
Islamic religious leaders of his time, Jinnah realized
that the state structure in post-independence India
would not be neutral and would favor those who
controlled it.

His leadership and strategies were not solely based on
religious motivations but were driven by political
considerations. Although he invoked Islam in his
political discourse, particularly after 1934 when he
began to reorganize the Muslim League, he employed
Islamic references more as a means of political
mobilization and as a unifier among Muslims with

diverse linguistic and regional backgrounds. Islam, in Jinnah's vision, was a common denominator among Indian Muslims, which he used effectively to mobilize support for the Muslim League, especially in the 1946 provincial elections.

Jinnah's vision for Pakistan was not that of a religious or orthodox Islamic state. His political career and the contents of the Lucknow Pact (1916), his 14 points (1929), and his role during the first and second Roundtable Conferences (1930-31) all pointed towards securing the political, economic, and cultural interests of Muslims. The establishment of Pakistan, as per Jinnah's vision, was based on these political considerations rather than religious ones.

Moreover, Jinnah's emphasis on the protection of the rights, religion, and cultures of minorities in the new state of Pakistan was evident. He assured religious minorities of equal citizenship and non-discrimination by the state on the basis of religion, caste, or creed. In his view, Islamic ideals and principles could be reconciled with the imperatives of a modern state, democracy, the rule of law, and civil and political rights

Jinnah's leadership during this tumultuous period was thus characterized by his ability to navigate complex political landscapes, his use of Islam as a unifying force rather than a strict legal code, and his vision of a modern, inclusive state that respected the rights and identities of all its citizens.

The challenges of nation-building

The challenges of nation-building in the aftermath of the Partition of India in 1947, which led to the creation of two independent dominions, India and Pakistan, were multifaceted and profound. This period was marked by a multitude of difficulties, ranging from political and administrative hurdles to social and economic crises. The task of creating a new nation, especially under the complex circumstances that Pakistan faced, was colossal. We'll explore these challenges in depth, weaving in examples and lesser-known facts to provide a comprehensive understanding.

1. Political and Administrative Challenges
a. Establishing Governance Structures
Formation of Government: Pakistan had to rapidly establish a functional government. Muhammad Ali Jinnah, as the first Governor-General, faced the daunting task of setting up a new administrative framework.
Lack of Experienced Personnel: There was a significant dearth of trained civil servants and administrators, as many experienced officials chose to remain in India.
b. Territorial Disputes and Integration
Kashmir Conflict: The unresolved status of Kashmir became a persistent source of conflict with India.
Integration of Princely States: Integrating princely states like Balochistan posed significant political challenges.
2. Refugee Crisis and Social Challenges
a. Handling Massive Migration
Unprecedented Migration: The partition led to one of the largest migrations in human history, with millions of people moving across the new borders.

Communal Violence: This migration was accompanied by horrific communal violence, exacerbating the refugee crisis.

b. Rehabilitation and Settlement

Shelter and Basic Needs: Providing shelter and basic necessities to millions of refugees was a herculean task.

Social Integration: Fostering a sense of national identity among diverse groups coming from different regions was challenging.

3. Economic and Resource Challenges

a. Infrastructure and Economic Development

Lack of Industrial Base: Pakistan inherited a limited industrial base, requiring significant efforts to build its economy.

Agricultural Challenges: Partition disrupted agricultural activities, especially in Punjab, the breadbasket of the region.

b. Financial Instability

Division of Assets: The division of financial assets and liabilities with India was contentious and complicated.

Foreign Aid and Loans: Pakistan had to rely heavily on foreign aid and loans to stabilize its economy.

4. Security and Defense Concerns

a. Building a Military

Division of Military Assets: The allocation of military assets between India and Pakistan was a contentious issue, leading to an imbalance.

External Threats: The young nation had to immediately address security concerns, particularly from its larger neighbor, India.

b. Internal Security

Communal Riots: Managing communal tensions within the country was a persistent issue.

Regional Insurgencies: Tackling insurgencies and regional discontent, especially in areas like East

Pakistan (later Bangladesh), required significant attention.

5. Cultural and Identity Formation

a. Creating a National Identity

Religious and Ethnic Diversity: Balancing the diverse religious and ethnic composition of the population while promoting a unified Pakistani identity was a complex task.

Language Controversy: The decision to adopt Urdu as the national language led to discontent, especially in East Pakistan.

b. Education and Cultural Development

Building an Education System: Establishing a national education system that catered to the needs of a diverse population was crucial.

Promotion of Arts and Culture: Cultivating a unique cultural identity through arts and literature was part of the nation-building process.

Conclusion

The journey of nation-building for Pakistan in the aftermath of the Partition was fraught with challenges that tested the resilience and determination of its people and leaders. It was a period marked by upheaval and hardship, but also one of hope and immense effort towards laying the foundations of a new nation. This complex tapestry of political, social, economic, and cultural challenges underscores the intricate process of creating a country from the throes of partition and conflict.

The story of Pakistan's early years is a testament to the strength and perseverance required in the face of overwhelming odds. It is a narrative that not only reflects the struggles specific to Pakistan but also offers universal insights into the challenges of nation-building in a post-colonial context.

Chapter 10: Founding Father of Pakistan

Jinnah's role as the founding father of Pakistan

Muhammad Ali Jinnah, revered as Quaid-e-Azam (Great Leader) in Pakistan, stands as a monumental figure in the annals of South Asian history. His journey from a young barrister in Bombay to the founding father of Pakistan is a tale of relentless perseverance, political acumen, and an unwavering vision for a separate homeland for Muslims in the Indian subcontinent. This narrative delves into Jinnah's multifaceted role in the creation of Pakistan, exploring his leadership, ideology, challenges, and his enduring legacy.

Early Life and Legal Career: The Foundation of a Visionary Leader

Jinnah's early life laid the groundwork for his future leadership. Born on December 25, 1876, in Karachi, he was educated at the Sindh Madressatul Islam and the Christian Mission School. A stint in London for legal studies at Lincoln's Inn not only shaped his legal acumen but also exposed him to the political ideas fermenting in Europe, notably nationalism and self-determination. His return to India and subsequent successful legal career in Bombay provided him with a platform to enter the political arena.

Political Ascendancy: From Indian National Congress to Muslim League

Jinnah initially joined the Indian National Congress, advocating for Hindu-Muslim unity and constitutional reforms under British rule. However, his perspective evolved with the growing realization that Congress was predominantly representing Hindu interests. This led to his pivotal shift to the All-India Muslim League in 1913. His transformation from an ambassador of Hindu-Muslim unity to a staunch advocate of Muslim separatism was not abrupt but a gradual response to the political dynamics of the time.

The Turning Point: Demand for Pakistan

The Lahore Resolution of 1940, under Jinnah's leadership, marked a decisive turn. Here, Jinnah articulated the demand for separate Muslim-majority states in the north-western and eastern zones of India. This was a radical shift from seeking minority protection to demanding sovereign nationhood. The resolution laid the foundation for Pakistan, a homeland for Muslims, where they could practice their religion and culture freely.

Strategic Leadership and Diplomacy

Jinnah's leadership was characterized by his strategic foresight and diplomatic skill. He adeptly navigated the complex political landscape, balancing the demands of various Muslim factions, countering Congress's opposition, and negotiating with the British rulers. His relentless advocacy for the Muslim cause earned him the title of Quaid-e-Azam.

The Partition and Its Aftermath

The culmination of Jinnah's efforts was the creation of Pakistan on August 14, 1947. However, the joy of independence was marred by the communal violence that accompanied the partition of India. Jinnah, as Pakistan's first Governor-General, faced the colossal task of establishing a new government, managing massive refugee influx, and laying down the foundations of a new country.

Jinnah's Vision for Pakistan

Jinnah envisioned Pakistan as a secular state where religion would not dictate state policy, a vision often debated and contested in the country's later years. He aspired for a nation where all citizens, irrespective of religion, would be equal.

Challenges and Criticisms

Jinnah's role as the architect of Pakistan is not without criticism. His critics argue that his demand for a separate Muslim state sowed the seeds of communal division and conflict in the subcontinent. The human cost of partition, with its unprecedented scale of violence and displacement, is often attributed to the hasty and ill-planned division of the country.

Legacy and Enduring Influence

Jinnah's legacy is multifaceted. In Pakistan, he is hailed as the father of the nation, his vision and leadership celebrated. His portrait adorns government offices, and his speeches and quotes are often invoked to inspire nationalism. Internationally, he is recognized as a key figure in the struggle against colonialism and for his role in shaping the post-colonial South Asian political landscape.

In conclusion, Muhammad Ali Jinnah's journey from a legal luminary to the founding father of Pakistan encapsulates a remarkable blend of vision, leadership, and political acumen. His role in the creation of Pakistan is a testament to his unwavering commitment to his cause, a journey marked by challenges, controversies, and enduring influence on the nation's identity and history. His life and legacy continue to evoke admiration, debate, and introspection, not just in Pakistan but across the world.

Jinnah's contributions to the establishment of the new nation

Muhammad Ali Jinnah, fondly remembered as the 'Quaid-e-Azam' or 'Great Leader,' played a pivotal role in the establishment of Pakistan, a nation forged on the principles of Muslim identity and self-determination. His journey from a young barrister to the founder of a nation is a tapestry woven with relentless determination, political acumen, and an unwavering vision. This narrative seeks to unravel the multifaceted contributions of Jinnah in sculpting the contours of the newly formed nation of Pakistan.

Early Advocacy and Political Foundations:
Jinnah's initial foray into politics was marked by his belief in Hindu-Muslim unity. His involvement in the Indian National Congress, where he was seen as the ambassador of Hindu-Muslim unity, laid the groundwork for his future leadership. However, as the political landscape evolved, Jinnah's perspectives underwent a metamorphosis, driven by the growing realization that Muslim interests could be overshadowed in a predominantly Hindu India.

Transition to Muslim League and the Two-Nation Theory:
The pivotal shift in Jinnah's political odyssey occurred with his deepening involvement in the All-India Muslim League. His articulation of the Two-Nation Theory, positing that Muslims and Hindus were distinct nations, with unbridgeable differences, became the bedrock of his quest for Pakistan. His eloquence, combined with his legal acumen, enabled him to frame

the demand for Pakistan in a manner that was both pragmatic and resonant with the Muslim masses.

The Lahore Resolution and the Path to Partition:
The Lahore Resolution of 1940, under Jinnah's stewardship, marked a definitive moment in the history of the Indian subcontinent. This resolution, later known as the 'Pakistan Resolution,' called for independent states in the northwestern and eastern areas of India, where Muslims were a majority. Jinnah's persuasive oratory and strategic politicking played a crucial role in transforming this vision into a mass movement.

Diplomatic Maneuvering and Negotiations:
Jinnah's diplomatic skills were evident in his negotiations with both the British government and the Indian National Congress. His ability to maintain a firm stance on Pakistan's demand, while navigating complex political negotiations, especially during the Simla Conference and the Round Table Conferences, was instrumental in the eventual realization of Pakistan.

Leadership During the Partition:
The partition of India, accompanied by communal riots and massive population transfers, presented monumental challenges. Jinnah, as the leader of the newly formed Pakistan, demonstrated exceptional leadership in addressing the refugee crisis, laying the foundations of a new government, and setting the tone for Pakistan's future.

Secular Vision and Governance:
Despite his advocacy for a Muslim-majority nation, Jinnah envisioned Pakistan as a secular state where religion would not dictate statecraft. His inaugural address to the Constituent Assembly of Pakistan on

August 11, 1947, where he emphasized the principle of equality regardless of religion or creed, stands as a testament to his secular ideals.

Promotion of Women's Rights:
Jinnah was also a proponent of women's rights in a predominantly patriarchal society. He encouraged women to participate in the national movement and in the building of the nation, a stance that was progressive for his time.

Legacy and Influence:
Jinnah's legacy is a complex tapestry of resilience, vision, and controversy. His contributions to the creation of Pakistan are unparalleled, yet his vision for the country has been a subject of extensive debate and interpretation in the years following his death.

In sum, Muhammad Ali Jinnah's role in the establishment of Pakistan was multifaceted, encompassing his transformation from a proponent of Hindu-Muslim unity to the architect of a separate nation for Muslims. His journey was marked by his exceptional legal prowess, strategic political maneuvers, and an unwavering commitment to his cause. His vision and actions laid the groundwork for the creation of Pakistan, impacting the geopolitical landscape of South Asia profoundly and irreversibly.

Jinnah's vision for Pakistan

Muhammad Ali Jinnah, a name etched in the annals of history, is celebrated as the architect of Pakistan's independence. His vision for the newly formed nation was not just a blueprint for political autonomy but a comprehensive framework encompassing various aspects of nation-building. Let's explore the multifarious dimensions of Jinnah's vision, which continue to resonate in the political and social fabric of Pakistan.

Political Sovereignty: A Dream of Independence
Jinnah's paramount objective was the political self-determination for Muslims in South Asia. He aspired for a nation where Muslims could govern their destiny, free from the fears of being overshadowed in a Hindu-majority India post-British rule. He imagined Pakistan as a sanctuary of political freedom and self-governance for Muslims.

Secularism: The Cornerstone of a New Nation
Contrary to common misconceptions, Jinnah did not envision Pakistan as a theocratic state. He dreamt of a secular Pakistan, where religion was a personal, not state affair. He aspired for a nation where mosques, temples, and churches stood side by side, symbolizing a pluralistic society. This secular vision was eloquently expressed in his address on August 11, 1947, where he emphasized religious freedom.

Democratic Ideals and the Rule of Law
Jinnah was a proponent of democratic principles and governance through the rule of law. He envisaged a Pakistan anchored in democracy, where the rights of minorities were protected and upheld. His vision was

for a country governed by laws, not individuals, ensuring equality and justice for all citizens.

Economic Prosperity and Social Equity
Jinnah's vision extended beyond politics into the realms of economic and social welfare. He dreamed of a prosperous Pakistan where wealth was not concentrated in the hands of a few but distributed equitably. He emphasized the importance of education, healthcare, and social services, aspiring for a nation where every individual had the opportunity to contribute to and benefit from economic growth.

Cultural Cohesion and National Identity
Jinnah recognized the diverse tapestry of cultures, languages, and ethnicities in Pakistan. He aimed to foster a sense of national unity that transcended these differences. He believed in a Pakistani identity that was inclusive, embracing the various cultural strands that made up the nation.

A Peaceful Stance in International Relations
Jinnah envisioned Pakistan as a peace-loving nation, committed to maintaining harmonious relations with its neighbors and the global community. He saw Pakistan as a responsible member of the international community, particularly within the Muslim world, advocating for peace and cooperation.

Reflecting on Challenges and Criticisms
However, Jinnah's vision was not without its challenges and controversies. The partition of India, which led to the creation of Pakistan, was marked by significant bloodshed and upheaval. This period of violence was a stark contradiction to Jinnah's ideals of peaceful coexistence. Critics have often pointed out the paradox

in creating a nation based on religious identity while advocating for secularism.

The Legacy and Its Interpretation
Over the years, Jinnah's vision has been subject to various interpretations, often molded to suit the political narratives of different eras in Pakistan. The secular elements of his vision have frequently been overshadowed by religious interpretations, fueling debates about Pakistan's true identity.

In Conclusion
Muhammad Ali Jinnah's vision for Pakistan was a complex interplay of ideals, encompassing autonomy, secular governance, democracy, economic prosperity, social justice, cultural unity, and peaceful international relations. His legacy, a subject of ongoing debate and inspiration, continues to influence the nation's quest for identity and purpose in the global arena. Jinnah's dream for Pakistan remains a guiding beacon, albeit one interpreted through various lenses over the decades.

His Efforts to shape its political, social, and economic trajectory

Muhammad Ali Jinnah, a figure of monumental significance in South Asian history, orchestrated the creation of Pakistan, a country born out of ideological and political necessity. His efforts in shaping Pakistan's political, social, and economic trajectory were profound, multifaceted, and continue to resonate in the nation's ethos. This exploration delves into these three key aspects, weaving through the intricate tapestry of Jinnah's indelible legacy.

1. Political Orchestration

Jinnah's political journey was a masterclass in strategy and resilience. Initially an ardent advocate for Hindu-Muslim unity within a united India, his disillusionment with Congress's policies led him to envisage Pakistan as a separate homeland for Muslims. This political volte-face was not abrupt but evolved through a complex interplay of events, negotiations, and realizations.

The Lahore Resolution (1940)

The Lahore Resolution in 1940, under Jinnah's stewardship, marked a definitive turn. Here, he articulated the demand for independent states for Muslims in the northwest and east of India. This resolution was a political masterstroke, setting the stage for the partition of India and the creation of Pakistan.

Negotiations and Diplomacy

Jinnah's negotiation skills were pivotal in dealing with the British and the Congress. His ability to maintain a firm stance on Pakistan's creation, coupled with his diplomatic tact, won him the title of 'Quaid-e-Azam' or

'Great Leader.' His political acumen was evident in the way he navigated the complex tapestry of colonial politics, communal interests, and international relations.

2. Social Fabric and Identity
Jinnah's influence on the social fabric of Pakistan was rooted in his vision of a progressive Muslim society. His speeches and policies reflected a desire for a pluralistic society, albeit anchored in Islamic principles.

Vision of a Progressive Society
Jinnah envisioned Pakistan as a progressive Muslim state, where religious freedom and social justice were paramount. He famously declared in a speech to the Constituent Assembly in August 1947 that citizens of any religion or caste would be treated equally, highlighting his commitment to a pluralistic and inclusive Pakistan.

Women Empowerment
He was a proponent of women's rights and empowerment. Jinnah believed that women were essential in the nation-building process and supported their participation in public and political life.

3. Economic Foundations
Economically, Jinnah's vision for Pakistan was of a self-sufficient state with robust agriculture and burgeoning industry. However, the immediate post-partition period was fraught with challenges, and Jinnah's untimely death left the task of economic consolidation unfinished.

Agriculture and Industry
Jinnah realized the importance of agriculture in Pakistan's economy and advocated for reforms to boost

agricultural productivity. Additionally, he saw industrial development as vital for economic independence and encouraged policies to foster industrial growth.

Trade and Commerce
Understanding the importance of trade, Jinnah promoted international commerce, aiming to establish Pakistan as a major trading hub in South Asia. His vision encompassed the development of infrastructure and policies conducive to trade and commerce.

Conclusion
Muhammad Ali Jinnah's role in shaping Pakistan's political, social, and economic trajectory was monumental. He navigated complex political landscapes, advocated for a progressive and inclusive society, and laid the groundwork for economic development. While his life was a testament to his visionary leadership, his death left a vacuum that challenged the nascent nation's stability and growth. Jinnah's legacy, however, continues to be a guiding beacon for Pakistan, inspiring generations with his unwavering commitment to the ideals of freedom, justice, and equality.

Chapter 11: Constitutional Debates and Challenges

Constitutional debates

The constitutional debates during Muhammad Ali Jinnah's tenure as the founder of Pakistan were deeply intertwined with the vision he had for the newly formed nation. Jinnah's outlook on Pakistan's identity and governance structure was complex and evolved over time, influenced by the political and communal dynamics of the era.

Jinnah, initially a proponent of Hindu-Muslim unity, experienced a shift in his political stance over the years. This change is evident in his speeches and actions leading up to and following the creation of Pakistan. In a speech in the Central Legislative Assembly in 1935, Jinnah emphasized that religion should not intrude into politics, and issues concerning minorities were essentially political. His views were further nuanced by his remarks to students at the Ismaili College in Bombay in 1943, where he stated that while no government should interfere with religion, the Muslims were a distinct nation from the Hindus.

The constitutional debates during Jinnah's time were marked by his insistence on the political rights of Muslims as a distinct community. This stance was a critical factor in the eventual creation of Pakistan. Jinnah's vision of Pakistan was initially not of an Islamic state but more of a state with a Muslim majority where Muslims could exercise political and cultural autonomy. This vision was devoid of any explicit intention to establish an Islamic state, as seen in his speeches and particularly at the Lahore Session of the Muslim League in 1940.

Post-independence, the framing of Pakistan's constitution and the establishment of its political structure were influenced by Jinnah's ideals and the realities of the time. The 1956 Constitution of Pakistan, for instance, established a unicameral Parliament, consisting of the President and the National Assembly, with seats reserved for women and an equal division between East and West Pakistan. This structure reflected Jinnah's emphasis on a balanced representation of the diverse regions and communities within Pakistan.

However, Jinnah's vision faced challenges, and the early years of Pakistan were marked by political instability. The first general election was scheduled for 1959 but never occurred, as President Sikandar Mirza abrogated the Constitution and declared Martial Law in 1958. These events marked a deviation from Jinnah's original vision and highlighted the complexities of establishing a stable democratic framework in the nascent country.

In summary, the constitutional debates during Muhammad Ali Jinnah's tenure were characterized by his evolving political philosophy, a focus on the political rights and identity of Muslims, and the challenges of crafting a stable and representative governance structure in the face of regional, communal, and political complexities. His vision for Pakistan was multifaceted, shaped by the historical and political context of the time, and had a lasting impact on the country's constitutional and political development.

Challenges faced by Pakistan in its formative years

Muhammad Ali Jinnah, the founder and first Governor-General of Pakistan, faced numerous challenges in the formative years of the newly established country. His tenure, though brief, was marked by a series of complex issues that had a lasting impact on Pakistan's trajectory.

Ideological Divergence and Political Challenges: Initially aligned with the Indian National Congress (INC), Jinnah's relationship with the party deteriorated over time, primarily due to his disagreements with Gandhi's approach of non-cooperation and civil disobedience against the British. Jinnah believed this would lead to lawlessness, preferring constitutional reform and political negotiation instead. His concerns over the INC's approach to minority rights, particularly Muslims, eventually led him to depart from the INC and join the All India Muslim League, playing a pivotal role in its ascent.

The Demand for Separate Electorates and Muslim Representation: As a leader, Jinnah was deeply concerned about the representation and rights of Muslims within a Hindu-majority India. This concern led to the demand for separate electorates, a system where minorities could elect their representatives. The Lucknow Pact of 1916, an agreement between the INC and the Muslim League, was a significant step towards this goal, acknowledging the need for separate electorates for Muslims.

Pakistan's Foreign Policy Vision: Jinnah envisioned a foreign policy for Pakistan based on the principle of "enmity with none, and peace with all." This vision was reflective of his desire for Pakistan to maintain neutrality and foster peace in its international relations. However, historically, Pakistan has struggled to maintain this vision, often finding itself in conflict or aligned with major powers for strategic reasons.

Islamization and Departure from Jinnah's Vision: Post Jinnah's era, particularly from the 1970s under Zia ul-Haq, Pakistan underwent a process of Islamization. This shift marked a significant departure from Jinnah's vision of a secular Pakistan. The introduction of compulsory religious instruction and the promotion of conservative Islam in various aspects of society, including foreign policy, deviated from the secular and democratic ideals envisioned by Jinnah.

Degeneration of Democratic Institutions: The failure to establish a democratic culture within political parties led to the rise of a bureaucracy-military nexus, often resulting in military dictatorships. This undermined the democratic principles Jinnah had hoped to instill in Pakistan. The frequent military interventions in politics and governance further deviated the country from the path envisioned by its founder.

Vision of a Democratic State Based on Islamic Principles: Jinnah aspired for Pakistan to be a modern democratic state, with its foundation laid on Islamic principles and values. He envisioned a system that would ensure social economic justice and the rights of minorities, drawing inspiration from Islamic ethics for constitution-making and governance.

Jinnah's tenure and the subsequent years highlight the complexities of founding a new nation with diverse aspirations and challenges. His vision for Pakistan, though partially realized, continues to influence the country's political and social fabric.

Jinnah's efforts to navigate the complexities of nation-building

Muhammad Ali Jinnah, a figure both celebrated and controversial, stands as a titan in the history of the Indian subcontinent. His journey, marked by relentless ambition and a remarkable political acumen, led to the creation of a new nation—Pakistan. In exploring Jinnah's role in this unparalleled event, we delve into the labyrinth of nation-building, a task replete with formidable challenges and complex negotiations.

Early Stirrings: The Genesis of a Vision
Jinnah's political journey commenced within the fabric of the Indian National Congress, where he initially sought a united front against British rule. A barrister by profession, educated in the cosmopolitan milieu of London, Jinnah brought a unique blend of Western liberal thought and an unwavering commitment to India's cause. However, his initial vision of a united India began to diverge due to ideological rifts, especially concerning the representation and rights of Muslims in a predominantly Hindu society.

The Turn to Muslim Nationalism
The pivotal shift in Jinnah's political ideology is a study in the dynamics of identity politics and minority rights. His transformation from an ambassador of Hindu-Muslim unity to the proponent of a separate Muslim nation was gradual. The Lahore Resolution of 1940, which he orchestrated, marked the formal demand for a separate Muslim state. This was not merely a political maneuver but a seismic shift in the subcontinent's socio-political landscape, signifying the crystallization of Muslim nationalism.

Navigating the Partition and Its Aftermath
The partition of India in 1947, a direct outcome of
Jinnah's relentless advocacy for a Muslim homeland,
unleashed a cataclysm of communal violence and mass
migration. Jinnah, now the Governor-General of
Pakistan, faced the Herculean task of nation-building
amidst the chaos. He grappled with forming a
government, addressing the plight of millions of
refugees, and establishing Pakistan's international
identity. His vision of Pakistan, often declared in his
speeches, was of a secular state where religion would
not be the criterion for citizenship—a vision that, in
later years, would be contested and reinterpreted.

Economic and Administrative Foundations
An aspect often overshadowed in discussions about
Jinnah is his approach to economic and administrative
challenges. He laid the foundations of Pakistan's
administrative system and took steps to foster economic
independence. His policies were geared towards
creating a self-sufficient state that could withstand the
pressures of a partitioned economy. The creation of the
State Bank of Pakistan and the initiation of
infrastructural projects were steps towards this goal.

Diplomatic Maneuvering
In the arena of international politics, Jinnah
demonstrated remarkable acumen. He navigated the
complex geopolitics of the time, seeking to position
Pakistan as a sovereign entity on the global stage. His
efforts to secure Pakistan's membership in the United
Nations and establish diplomatic relations with other
countries were crucial in asserting Pakistan's
international presence.

The Legacy and Controversies

Jinnah's legacy is a tapestry of achievements and controversies. He is revered as the 'Father of the Nation' in Pakistan, yet his strategies and decisions, particularly regarding the partition and its violent aftermath, remain subjects of intense debate. The creation of Pakistan altered the geopolitical landscape of South Asia, and Jinnah's role in this transformation is both celebrated and critiqued.

Conclusion: The Complexity of Nation-Building

Jinnah's life and efforts in nation-building reflect the complexities and paradoxes inherent in such a colossal task. His story is one of a visionaries who, through a combination of political sagacity and unwavering determination, carved out a nation from the tumultuous fabric of colonial India. It is a narrative that underscores the challenges of identity, representation, and statecraft in a world grappling with the legacy of colonialism and the aspirations of diverse peoples.

In sum, Muhammad Ali Jinnah's journey in nation-building was marked by a series of strategic shifts, bold decisions, and an unyielding vision for a separate Muslim homeland. His legacy, layered and multifaceted, continues to inspire, influence, and provoke debate, underscoring the profound impact of his life and work on the history of the Indian subcontinent.

Framework for governance that reflected Jinnah's vision for the country

Muhammad Ali Jinnah's vision for Pakistan was complex and multifaceted, reflecting his diverse influences and the historical context in which he operated. Jinnah, a key figure in the creation of Pakistan, sought to establish a nation that would serve as a homeland for Muslims while also being inclusive, democratic, and fair to all its citizens.

One aspect of Jinnah's vision was to ensure political and religious freedom for all citizens, irrespective of their religion. In a speech on August 11, 1947, Jinnah emphasized the importance of religious liberty and equality, stating that citizens should be free to go to their temples, mosques, or other places of worship and that their religion or creed should not affect their citizenship rights.

Jinnah's approach to governance was also influenced by his legal background and his time in England. He envisioned Pakistan as a modern state, aspiring for it to be a leader not only in the Muslim world but globally in various fields like economy, science, technology, and education. His interpretation of Islam was progressive and enlightened, emphasizing the pluralistic spirit of Islam and its history of coexistence with other faiths. This vision was also shaped by British liberalism, which he absorbed during his education as a barrister in England.

Despite these ideals, Jinnah's vision for Pakistan has been a subject of debate and interpretation. While he emphasized inclusivity and democracy, he also saw Pakistan as a state for Muslims, with Shariah as a source and inspiration for law and constitution. However, this did not imply a preference for a theocracy. The complexity lies in his understanding of what a 'Muslim democracy' could be and how it would treat its minorities. His idea of Islam differed significantly from the views held by religious clerics and fundamentalists, and he strongly opposed the notion of a theocracy.

Jinnah's political journey and the events leading to the creation of Pakistan also reflect his commitment to Muslim representation and rights within the subcontinent's political landscape. His involvement in various political activities, such as the Lucknow Pact and the reorganization of the Muslim League, showcased his efforts to ensure effective representation for Muslims while also striving for harmony and equality among all communities.

Jinnah's vision and the path he charted for Pakistan were rooted in a complex interplay of historical, political, and religious factors. His dream was for a prosperous, tolerant nation where all citizens, regardless of their background, could live in harmony and with equal rights. However, the nuances of his vision have led to various interpretations and debates about the nature of the state he intended to create.

Chapter 12: Legacy of Leadership

Jinnah's leadership style

Muhammad Ali Jinnah, a pivotal figure in the history
of South Asia, is widely acclaimed for his instrumental
role in the creation of Pakistan. His leadership style,
marked by its complexity and evolution over time,
merits a comprehensive analysis. This exploration
delves into various facets of Jinnah's leadership,
encompassing his early political involvement,
transformational phases, strategic acumen, and
enduring impact.

Early Political Involvement
Born on December 25, 1876, in Karachi, Jinnah
initially embarked on a legal career in England. His
early political inclinations were moderate, aligning with
the Indian National Congress's aspirations for greater
self-governance within the British Empire. Jinnah's
initial approach was characterized by constitutionalism,
advocating legal and systematic reforms rather than
direct confrontation.

Transformational Leadership
Jinnah's leadership underwent significant
transformation. Initially an advocate of Hindu-Muslim
unity, he later pivoted towards an unwavering stand for
a separate Muslim nation. This shift was not abrupt but
evolved through personal experiences and political
developments. His disillusionment with Congress's
stance on Muslim issues, particularly after the Nehru
Report (1928), which ignored Muslim political rights,
catalyzed his transformation.

Strategic Acumen and Vision
Jinnah's leadership was marked by a remarkable strategic acumen. He possessed the foresight to anticipate political developments and the tactical brilliance to navigate complex negotiations. His vision for Pakistan was not just as a refuge for South Asia's Muslims but as a progressive, democratic nation. Jinnah's insistence on a separate state was not merely a response to communal tensions but a strategic move to secure Muslims' political, cultural, and economic rights.

Diplomatic Skills and Determination
Jinnah's diplomatic skills were evident in his dealings with both British authorities and opposing Indian political leaders. His approach was firm yet pragmatic, balancing idealism with realism. His unwavering determination, often seen as obstinacy, was a key factor in achieving his objectives. He navigated through various rounds of negotiations and proposals, such as the Cabinet Mission Plan and the Lahore Resolution, with a clear vision and steadfastness.

Enduring Impact and Controversies
Jinnah's leadership style and decisions have been subjects of extensive debate. Critics argue that his demand for Pakistan deepened communal divisions, while supporters view him as a savior of Muslims' rights in the Indian subcontinent. His vision for Pakistan, particularly his speech on August 11, 1947, advocating for a secular state where religion would be separate from state affairs, remains a subject of interpretation and debate.

Conclusion
Muhammad Ali Jinnah's leadership style was a blend of constitutionalism, transformational vision, strategic

brilliance, and unyielding determination. His journey from a proponent of Hindu-Muslim unity to the architect of a separate Muslim nation exemplifies a complex and adaptive leadership approach. His legacy, shrouded in admiration and controversy, continues to influence political discourse in South Asia.

This analysis, while extensive, only scratches the surface of Jinnah's multifaceted leadership style. His role as the founder of Pakistan and a key figure in the subcontinent's partition saga remains a rich subject for study and reflection, offering insights into the complexities of leadership in tumultuous times.

Jinnah's political philosophy

Analyzing the political philosophy of Muhammad Ali Jinnah, the founder of Pakistan, requires delving into the complex tapestry of historical, cultural, and personal influences that shaped his political ideology. Jinnah, a figure of monumental significance in South Asian history, was a man of contrasts and contradictions, whose political journey was marked by a remarkable evolution.

Early Influences and Legal Background
Born in 1876, Jinnah's formative years were during the height of British colonial rule in India. His education in England and early career as a lawyer significantly influenced his political philosophy. Trained in the British legal system, he developed a strong belief in the rule of law, constitutionalism, and parliamentary democracy. These principles were evident throughout his political career.

Initial Foray into Politics: Moderate and Constitutionalist
Jinnah initially emerged as a moderate in the Indian National Congress, advocating for Hindu-Muslim unity and constitutional reforms within the British Empire. His approach was pragmatic and constitutionalist, focusing on legal avenues and gradual reforms rather than radical change.

Shift Towards Muslim Nationalism
The turning point in Jinnah's political philosophy came in the 1930s. Frustrated by the Congress's perceived inability to protect Muslim interests, he gravitated towards the idea that Muslims in India were not just a minority but a distinct nation. This marked his

transition from a pan-Indian nationalist to a Muslim nationalist, leading to his eventual demand for a separate Muslim state, Pakistan.

The Two-Nation Theory

Jinnah's adoption of the Two-Nation Theory was pivotal. He argued that Hindus and Muslims were not just religious groups but two separate nations, with distinct cultures, traditions, and social laws. This theory became the bedrock of his demand for Pakistan and was a radical departure from the earlier secular-nationalist approach that sought to accommodate diverse groups within a single Indian state.

Democratic Ideals and Secularism

Despite his advocacy for a Muslim state, Jinnah's vision of Pakistan was not theocratic. He envisioned a secular Pakistan where religion would not be the basis for the state's governance. His famous speech on August 11, 1947, highlighted his commitment to a secular and inclusive Pakistan where all citizens, regardless of religion, would be equal.

Realpolitik and Pragmatism

Jinnah's political philosophy was also marked by a strong sense of realpolitik. He was a pragmatic leader, often willing to compromise and negotiate to achieve his goals. His ability to maneuver through the complex political landscape of the time, balancing between the British authorities, the Congress, and various Muslim factions, was a testament to his political acumen.

Conclusion: A Complex Legacy

Jinnah's political philosophy was a blend of liberalism, secularism, and nationalism, tempered by realism and pragmatism. It evolved over time, shaped by the tumultuous context of his era. While his advocacy for Pakistan's creation was rooted in the protection of Muslim interests, his vision for the state was progressive and secular. This complexity makes Jinnah a fascinating, if sometimes contradictory, figure in the annals of political thought. His legacy continues to influence the political discourse in both Pakistan and India, reflecting the enduring impact of his visionary yet pragmatic approach to politics.

Jinnah's enduring impact on the trajectory of Pakistan

Muhammad Ali Jinnah, the founding father of
Pakistan, left an indelible mark on the country's
trajectory, shaping its political, cultural, and societal
landscapes. This analysis aims to delve deeply into
Jinnah's enduring impact on Pakistan, exploring the
multifaceted dimensions of his legacy.

I. Political Architecture and Governance
A. Establishment of a Sovereign State
Jinnah's foremost contribution was the creation of
Pakistan itself. Championing the cause of Muslim
nationalism, he transformed the All-India Muslim
League into a pivotal political force. The Lahore
Resolution of 1940, spearheaded by Jinnah, laid the
foundation for the demand for a separate Muslim-
majority nation, culminating in the partition of India in
1947.

B. Democratic Ideals and Constitutional Framework
Jinnah envisioned Pakistan as a democratic entity with
a strong emphasis on the rule of law. His address to the
Constituent Assembly on August 11, 1947, underscored
his commitment to an inclusive, egalitarian society,
irrespective of religion or caste. This vision, though
contested and often deviated from in subsequent years,
continues to resonate in Pakistan's constitutional
aspirations and political debates.

II. Social and Cultural Fabric
A. Secularism vs. Islamic Identity
Jinnah's legacy in shaping Pakistan's identity is
complex. He envisaged a nation where Muslims could

practice their faith freely yet advocated for a secular state with religious neutrality. This duality continues to influence Pakistan's social fabric, oscillating between secular policies and Islamic principles.

B. National Unity and Ethnic Diversity
Jinnah's struggle for Pakistan was also a struggle for the unity of disparate Muslim communities. His vision of unity transcends ethnic and linguistic boundaries, striving for a cohesive national identity. However, the balancing act between a unified national identity and the recognition of diverse ethnic groups remains a challenge for Pakistan.

III. Economic Directions
A. Foundations for Economic Policy
Jinnah's economic vision for Pakistan was progressive. He supported free enterprise but also emphasized the need for social justice and equitable distribution of wealth. This dual approach laid the groundwork for Pakistan's economic policies, oscillating between socialist and capitalist models over the years.

B. Industrial and Agricultural Development
Under Jinnah's guidance, the initial focus was on industrialization and agricultural development. His policies aimed at self-sufficiency, particularly in the agriculture sector, which remains a cornerstone of Pakistan's economy.

IV. Foreign Policy and International Relations
A. Non-Aligned Movement and Global Positioning
Jinnah's foreign policy was marked by neutrality and non-alignment, as he sought to position Pakistan as a moderate player in the international arena. This

approach has influenced Pakistan's foreign relations, particularly during the Cold War era.

B. Relations with Neighbors
Jinnah advocated for peaceful relations with neighboring countries, including India. His approach towards resolving issues like the Kashmir dispute was based on legal and peaceful methods. The Indo-Pak relationship today still navigates the complex legacy left by Jinnah.

V. Education and Intellectual Development
A. Emphasis on Education
Jinnah stressed the importance of education as a means of national development. His vision for an educated populace has influenced Pakistan's educational policies, focusing on literacy and higher education as tools for socio-economic progress.

Conclusion
Muhammad Ali Jinnah's impact on Pakistan is profound and multi-dimensional. His vision and actions laid the foundations of a nation that continues to evolve. While some of his ideals have been fully embraced, others remain aspirational, guiding the nation's journey. Jinnah's legacy is a tapestry of political foresight, cultural pluralism, economic ambition, and an unwavering commitment to the idea of Pakistan, serving as a beacon for its future trajectory.

This analysis, while extensive, touches just the surface of Jinnah's comprehensive influence on Pakistan. His legacy is not only historical but also a living guide, shaping the country's ongoing narrative.

Jinnah's legacy as a statesman

Muhammad Ali Jinnah, revered as the founder of Pakistan, carved a niche for himself in the annals of history with his unparalleled statesmanship and unwavering commitment to his cause. This exploration of his legacy delves into the multifaceted dimensions of his life and leadership, underscoring his enduring influence.

Early Life and Legal Career
Born on December 25, 1876, in Karachi, Jinnah's journey from a young barrister to a political colossus was marked by relentless perseverance. Educated in England, his legal acumen, developed during his years at Lincoln's Inn, laid the foundation for his future political endeavors. He returned to India equipped with a sharp legal mind and a vision for a just society.

Political Genesis
Jinnah's initial political leanings were towards a unified, independent India, where Hindus and Muslims coexisted harmoniously. His membership in the Indian National Congress (INC) and later, his pivotal role in the All-India Muslim League (AIML), underscored a gradual shift in his ideology, driven by the rising tide of religious and cultural discord.

The Turning Point: Demand for Pakistan
The Lahore Resolution of 1940, a milestone in South Asian history, marked Jinnah's unequivocal demand for a separate nation for Muslims. This momentous shift was not just a political maneuver but a response to the deep-seated religious divisions and fears of minority oppression. Jinnah's vision for Pakistan was rooted in

the desire for a land where Muslims could practice their faith and culture freely.

Jinnah's Statesmanship
Jinnah's statesmanship was characterized by his strategic acumen, legal prowess, and indomitable will. His negotiations with the British government and Hindu leaders were marked by his steadfastness and eloquence. His ability to maneuver through complex political landscapes, while maintaining his principles, was a testament to his exceptional leadership.

The Creation of Pakistan
The partition of India in 1947 and the creation of Pakistan were the culmination of Jinnah's lifelong struggle. This historic event, albeit marred by communal violence, was a monumental achievement. Jinnah's role in this partition showcased his ability to achieve seemingly impossible goals through sheer determination and strategic foresight.

Jinnah's Vision for Pakistan
Jinnah envisaged Pakistan as a progressive, inclusive state. His inaugural address to the Constituent Assembly of Pakistan on August 11, 1947, emphasized religious freedom and equality. He dreamt of a nation where religion or belief would have nothing to do with the business of the state, underscoring his secular outlook.

Challenges and Criticisms
Jinnah's journey was not without challenges and criticisms. The partition of India led to one of the largest mass migrations in history, accompanied by horrific communal violence. Critics argue that Jinnah's steadfast pursuit of a separate Muslim state contributed

to this turmoil. However, his supporters view him as a savior of Muslim identity and rights in the subcontinent.

Jinnah's Legacy

Jinnah's legacy is a blend of admiration and controversy. In Pakistan, he is venerated as the 'Quaid-e-Azam' (Great Leader) and the 'Father of the Nation.' His vision, leadership, and unwavering commitment to his cause remain sources of inspiration. However, his role in the partition and its aftermath continues to be a subject of debate and analysis.

Conclusion

Muhammad Ali Jinnah's journey from a barrister to the founder of Pakistan is a narrative of resilience, vision, and exceptional statesmanship. His life reflects the complexities of colonial India and the turbulent path to independence. Jinnah's legacy, intertwined with the history of South Asia, continues to influence and inspire generations, offering profound insights into leadership, perseverance, and the power of conviction.

Jinnah's legacy as a visionary leader

Exploring the legacy of Muhammad Ali Jinnah, the revered founder of Pakistan, requires delving into the multifaceted aspects of his life and leadership. This exploration will not only highlight his vision and foresight but also illuminate the rare aspects of his personality and governance that have left an indelible mark on the history and identity of Pakistan.

Early Years: The Formative Influence
Born on December 25, 1876, in Karachi, Jinnah's early life was marked by conventional education, but it was his time in London that significantly shaped his worldview. His exposure to Western liberal thought and legal education at Lincoln's Inn cultivated in him a blend of Eastern values and Western pragmatism. This unique amalgamation of cultures profoundly influenced his political ideology and leadership style.

The Legal Luminary: Foundation of Political Insight
Jinnah's return to India saw him establish himself as a successful lawyer. However, his legal career was more than a professional achievement; it was the crucible in which his political acumen was forged. His advocacy for legal justice transitioned seamlessly into a fight for political justice, especially for the Muslim community in India.

Political Evolution: From Unity to Partition
Initially an ardent supporter of Hindu-Muslim unity within the Indian National Congress, Jinnah's political journey underwent a significant transformation. His vision evolved from seeking constitutional reforms

within the British Indian Empire to championing the cause of a separate nation for Muslims. This shift was not impulsive but a response to the deepening communal divide and the failure of the Congress to address Muslim concerns adequately.

Visionary Leadership: The Demand for Pakistan
Jinnah's demand for Pakistan was rooted in his deep understanding of the Indian socio-political landscape. He foresaw the potential communal discord in a united India post-independence. His vision was not merely a reaction to immediate circumstances but a strategic foresight into the future of the subcontinent. His relentless advocacy for Pakistan was a testament to his extraordinary leadership and unwavering commitment to the Muslim cause.

The Lahore Resolution: A Milestone
The 1940 Lahore Resolution, commonly known as the Pakistan Resolution, was a pivotal moment in Jinnah's political journey and in the history of South Asia. This resolution marked the formal call for a separate Muslim homeland, encapsulating Jinnah's vision. It was his leadership that transformed the idea of Pakistan from a concept into a tangible goal.

Crafting a New Nation: Challenges and Achievements
Jinnah's role in the creation of Pakistan was just the beginning. As the new nation's first Governor-General, he faced the enormous task of establishing a functional government, managing the massive influx of refugees, and setting the foundation for a country that was conceived on the principles of Islamic social justice and democracy. His speeches and policies during this time reflect a leader striving to build a progressive and inclusive nation.

The Legacy: Beyond Politics

Jinnah's legacy extends beyond his political achievements. His personal attributes of integrity, eloquence, and a keen legal mind contributed significantly to his status as a revered leader. His vision for Pakistan – a modern, democratic state where all citizens, irrespective of religion or ethnicity, could coexist – continues to inspire.

Unseen Aspects: The Personal Side

Less discussed is Jinnah's personal life, which was marked by tragedies and challenges. His marriage to Rattanbai Petit and the subsequent death of their daughter Dina, and later Rattanbai herself, were profound personal losses that he bore with stoic resilience. These personal experiences, though rarely highlighted, played a role in shaping his character and leadership.

Criticisms and Controversies: A Balanced View

Jinnah's leadership was not without criticism. His detractors accused him of being overly rigid and blamed him for the partition's violence. However, a balanced view of history suggests that these criticisms oversimplify the complex realities of that era. Jinnah's strategies, often deemed controversial, were responses to the challenges he faced in a turbulent time.

Conclusion: The Enduring Vision:

Muhammad Ali Jinnah's journey from a young barrister to the founder of a nation is a testament to his visionary leadership. His ability to navigate through extraordinarily complex political landscapes and his unwavering commitment to his cause left an enduring legacy. Today, Jinnah's vision for Pakistan remains a guiding light, a source of inspiration for leaders and citizens alike in their pursuit of a progressive and harmonious society.

Jinnah's legacy as a symbol of unity for the Pakistani nation

Muhammad Ali Jinnah, the founder of Pakistan and affectionately known as Quaid-e-Azam (Great Leader), is a towering figure in the history of South Asia. His life and legacy have been a beacon of inspiration, a symbol of unity, and a subject of profound admiration for the Pakistani nation. This exploration delves into the multifaceted legacy of Jinnah, highlighting how his vision, leadership, and unyielding commitment to his principles helped forge a new nation and continue to serve as a unifying force for Pakistan.

Early Life and Legal Career: A Foundation of Excellence
Born on December 25, 1876, in Karachi, Jinnah's journey from a young barrister to the architect of a nation is a testament to his remarkable determination and intellectual prowess. Educated in London, Jinnah's legal career, first in Bombay and later across British India, was marked by his exceptional legal acumen and articulate advocacy. His early legal triumphs, often overshadowed by his political achievements, laid the foundation for his meticulous approach to leadership and governance.

The Political Metamorphosis: From Ambassador of Unity to Architect of Partition
Initially, Jinnah was a proponent of Hindu-Muslim unity, a member of both the Indian National Congress and the All-India Muslim League. His transformation from an ambassador of Hindu-Muslim unity to the proponent of a separate Muslim homeland is a complex narrative. Jinnah's disillusionment with the Congress's

stance towards Muslim concerns and the realization that a united India would not guarantee the rights and representation of Muslims catalyzed this shift. This period illustrates his adaptability and foresight in recognizing and responding to the evolving political landscape.

The Pakistan Movement: A Struggle for a Separate Nation
Jinnah's leadership in the Pakistan Movement from 1940, marked by the Lahore Resolution, until the creation of Pakistan on August 14, 1947, is an epoch of remarkable determination and political sagacity. His ability to galvanize the Muslim masses, unify diverse Muslim opinions, and navigate the complex negotiations with the British and the Congress, underscores his role as a unifying symbol. His speeches and writings from this period reflect a deep commitment to democracy, equality, and justice, values he envisioned for Pakistan.

The Vision for Pakistan: A Beacon of Hope and Unity
Jinnah's vision for Pakistan was far ahead of its time. He envisaged a nation where religion, culture, and ethnic differences were not just tolerated but celebrated. His inaugural address to the Constituent Assembly on August 11, 1947, encapsulates this vision, emphasizing religious freedom and equality. Jinnah's vision remains a cornerstone of Pakistan's identity and a unifying force, inspiring successive generations to strive for a progressive and inclusive nation.

Jinnah's Death and Enduring Legacy
Jinnah's untimely death on September 11, 1948, left the nascent nation bereft of its most charismatic leader. However, his legacy endures, transcending time and

continuing to serve as a symbol of unity for Pakistan. Jinnah's life is a narrative of resilience, a reminder of the power of conviction, and the importance of steadfastness in one's principles.

Reflections and Conclusion
Muhammad Ali Jinnah's life and legacy are not just the story of a man who created a nation; they are a testament to the enduring power of unity and vision. His journey from a legal luminary to the father of a nation, his transformation in political ideologies, and his unwavering commitment to his principles, all contribute to his iconic status. As Pakistan navigates the challenges of the 21st century, Jinnah's legacy as a symbol of unity continues to resonate, reminding its people of their shared history, aspirations, and destiny.

Jinnah's story is unique in the annals of history; a story that continues to inspire and unify a nation. His vision, determination, and sense of justice remain as relevant today as they were over seven decades ago, guiding Pakistan towards the realization of its full potential.

Chapter 13: Personal Life and Relationships

Jinnah's personal life

Muhammad Ali Jinnah, a figure of monumental significance in the history of South Asia, is often celebrated for his pivotal role in the creation of Pakistan. However, to truly understand this enigmatic leader, one must delve into the intricacies of his personal life, which paint a picture far more complex and human than the monolithic image of the 'Father of the Nation.'

Early Life and Education: A Precursor to Greatness

Born on December 25, 1876, in Karachi, then part of British India, Jinnah was the eldest of seven siblings in a prosperous merchant family. His early education at the Sindh-Madrasa-tul-Islam in Karachi, and later at the Christian Missionary Society High School, laid the foundation for his diverse and eclectic worldview.

Jinnah's journey to London in 1893 for further studies marked a turning point. He was called to the bar at Lincoln's Inn, making him one of the youngest Indians to achieve this feat. His time in England was not just an academic pursuit; it was a period of personal transformation. The exposure to Western philosophies and lifestyles significantly influenced his sartorial choices, eloquence, and legal acumen, aspects that became hallmarks of his personality.

Personal Life: The Man Behind the Leader

Jinnah's personal life was marked by tragedy and controversy. His marriage in 1918 to Rattanbai Petit, a Parsi who converted to Islam, was both a romantic and a societal defiance. The union, strained by religious and cultural differences, was short-lived with Rattanbai's untimely death in 1929, leaving behind their daughter, Dina. This loss cast a long shadow over Jinnah's life, adding to his aura of aloofness and solitude.

His relationship with his daughter Dina also became strained, especially after her marriage to a Parsi man, Neville Wadia. This personal heartache perhaps deepened his resolve for a separate Muslim nation, where religious and cultural identities could coexist without persecution or prejudice.

The Legal Luminary: A Glimpse into his Professional Prowess

Jinnah's legal career was as illustrious as his political journey. He was known for his meticulous preparation, exceptional memory, and eloquent oratory. One of his notable cases was the Bal Gangadhar Tilak sedition trial in 1916, where he earned acclaim for his spirited defense, highlighting his commitment to justice and civil liberties.

Lifestyle and Habits: The Quintessence of Discipline

Jinnah was a man of discipline and had a fondness for cigars and stylish attire. His wardrobe, always immaculate and western, was a symbol of his modern outlook and a break from traditional Indian attire. This sartorial elegance was not mere vanity but a calculated move to bridge cultures and present himself as a modern, forward-thinking leader.

Health Struggles: The Untold Battles

Behind the veneer of strength, Jinnah battled numerous health issues. His later years were marked by a worsening tuberculosis condition, a secret he guarded fiercely. His dedication to the cause of Pakistan's creation often came at the cost of his health, with him working tirelessly despite his worsening condition.

A Legacy Beyond Politics: Jinnah's Enduring Impact

Jinnah's personal life, with its triumphs and tribulations, shaped his political vision. His life is a testament to the power of resilience, the importance of personal convictions, and the impact of individual choices on historical trajectories. It is this human aspect of Jinnah, intertwined with his political legacy, that makes his biography a compelling narrative of a leader who was as much a product of his times as he was a shaper of them.

In conclusion, Muhammad Ali Jinnah's personal life offers a unique lens to view his public persona. It provides insights into the motivations, struggles, and convictions of a man who not only carved out a nation but also left an indelible mark on the tapestry of world history. His story is one of complexity, marked by personal loss, professional triumphs, and an unwavering commitment to his ideals, making him a figure of enduring interest and study.

Jinnah's family

Muhammad Ali Jinnah, born Mahomedali Jinnahbhai on December 25, 1876, in Karachi, was a prominent figure whose life and family background reflect a blend of tradition and modernity. Jinnah hailed from a family that belonged to the Ismaili Khoja creed of Shia Islam, though he later became a follower of the Twelver Shi'a teachings. His early education began at Sindh-Madrasa-tul-Islam, and later, he attended the Cathedral and John Connon School. His restless spirit took him to England at the age of 16, where he pursued law at Lincoln's Inn, becoming a barrister in 1895.

Jinnah's family life was marked by personal tragedies. He was married twice; his first wife, Emibai Jinnah, whom he married before leaving for England, died during his stay there. His second marriage was to Rattanbai Petit in 1918, but she also passed away in 1929. From his second marriage, he had a daughter named Dina Wadia, who was born in London in 1919. Dina's relationship with her father was strained due to her decision to marry a Parsi-born Indian, Neville Wadia, which led Jinnah to reportedly disown her.

Jinnah's early career as a lawyer in Bombay was noteworthy. He gained fame after fighting the 'Caucus Case' in 1907 and representing Bal Gangadhar Tilak, a prominent figure in the Indian National Congress, in 1908 and 1916. His political journey began with his involvement in the Indian National Congress in 1906. Jinnah was initially opposed to the idea of separate electorates for Muslims but eventually became a key figure in the Indian Independence movement, joining the All-India Muslim League in 1913 and playing a significant role in the signing of the Lucknow Pact in 1916, which aimed at Hindu–Muslim unity.

However, by the 1930s, Jinnah had become a central figure in the movement for a separate Muslim state in the Indian subcontinent, leading to the eventual creation of Pakistan in 1947, where he served as its first Governor-General until his death in 1948.

Jinnah's legacy is complex and multifaceted, reflecting his journey from a barrister to a political leader who played a pivotal role in the formation of Pakistan. His life story is a testament to the dynamic socio-political landscape of the Indian subcontinent during the early 20th century

Jinnah's relationships

Muhammad Ali Jinnah, the founder of Pakistan, had a complex and multi-faceted personal life, particularly concerning his relationships. His marriage to Rattanbai Petit, also known as Maryam, in 1918 was a significant event in his life. Rattanbai, who was 24 years younger than Jinnah, was the daughter of his personal friend Sir Dinshaw Petit and a member of the Parsi community. Before marrying Jinnah, she embraced Islam and changed her name to Maryam. The couple resided in Bombay and frequently traveled to Europe. In 1919, they had a daughter named Dina. However, Jinnah's marriage faced challenges, partly due to his intense focus on politics, which led to tensions in their relationship. The couple separated in 1927, and Rattanbai passed away after a serious illness.

Jinnah's relationship with his daughter, Dina Wadia, was also notable. Dina married Neville Wadia, a Parsi who had converted to Christianity, against Jinnah's wishes. This strained their relationship, leading Jinnah to become more formal with her, often addressing her as 'Mrs. Wadia'. However, it's reported that their relationship was not as formal as previously thought, as Dina's personal diary revealed a more affectionate side to their relationship. After her father's death, Dina visited Pakistan twice and maintained regular contact with her aunt, Fatima Jinnah.

Jinnah's personal life, especially his marriage to Rattanbai and his relationship with his daughter Dina, reflects the complex interplay of personal choices, cultural norms, and political ambitions that marked his life. His personal relationships, while often challenging, also reveal a more human side to a figure primarily known for his political leadership and vision for Pakistan.

Jinnah's personal struggles

Muhammad Ali Jinnah, revered as the founder of Pakistan, was not just a political leader; his life was a tapestry woven with personal struggles, dilemmas, and transformations. The narrative of his life is not just a tale of political triumph but also a story of personal evolution, challenges, and resilience. In exploring Jinnah's personal struggles, we delve into the lesser-known facets of his life, from his early days to his final years, revealing the human behind the statesman.

Early Life and Education: The Foundation of Resilience

Jinnah's journey began on December 25, 1876, in Karachi. Born into a mercantile family, he was exposed early on to the trials of business life. However, his personal struggle commenced when, as a teenager, he was sent to England for education. This was a period of immense transformation and challenge for young Jinnah. Imagine a young boy, unaccompanied and inexperienced, navigating the vastly different culture, climate, and educational system of Victorian England. It was here that Jinnah's resilience was forged, adapting to a foreign land while remaining steadfast in his cultural identity.

Early Career: Battling Prejudices and Professional Setbacks

Returning to India as a barrister, Jinnah entered the legal profession. Here, he faced the dual challenge of establishing himself in a competitive field while confronting the prejudices prevalent in colonial India. Despite being brilliant, he initially struggled to find his footing. It was his persistence and dedication that eventually led to his recognition as a leading lawyer.

Political Life: Ideological Shifts and Personal Loss

Jinnah's political life was marked by ideological shifts that reflected his personal struggles. Initially a member of the Indian National Congress, he believed in Hindu-Muslim unity. However, he gradually became disillusioned, realizing the stark realities of communal divisions. This ideological shift was not just political but deeply personal, reflecting his struggle to reconcile his vision with the evolving socio-political landscape of India.

Amidst his political journey, Jinnah faced profound personal loss. The death of his wife, Rattanbai Petit, was a blow that left him bereaved and lonely. This personal tragedy coincided with his growing disenchantment with Congress politics, leading him to take a hiatus from active politics. It was a period of introspection and re-evaluation, a testament to his ability to endure personal and political setbacks.

The Struggle for Pakistan: A Testament to Perseverance

The most significant struggle of Jinnah's life was the creation of Pakistan. It was an endeavor that demanded not just political acumen but immense personal sacrifice. He battled not only opposing political forces but also declining health. His unwavering commitment to his cause, even in the face of personal ailments, speaks volumes about his character.

Final Years: The Burden of Nation-Building

In the final years of his life, as the Governor-General of Pakistan, Jinnah faced the herculean task of nation-building. He grappled with administrative challenges, refugee crises, and the establishment of a new government. These were years marked by relentless work, often at the expense of his health.

Conclusion: The Legacy of Resilience and Determination

Jinnah's life was a testament to resilience. From a young student in England to the founder of a nation, his journey was fraught with personal and professional struggles. Yet, it is in these struggles that the essence of Jinnah's legacy lies: a legacy of perseverance, resilience, and an unwavering commitment to his principles. His life teaches us that personal struggles, no matter how daunting, can be the crucible for greatness.

Jinnah's personal experiences and his public role as a leader and statesman

Analyzing the intersection between Muhammad Ali Jinnah's personal experiences and his public role as a leader and statesman requires delving into the complex tapestry of his life, a journey where personal beliefs, circumstances, and decisions profoundly influenced his public persona and actions. This exploration, in its essence, is an attempt to understand how Jinnah's private world shaped his vision and strategies for the nation he helped birth - Pakistan.

Early Influences and Education
Jinnah's early life was marked by a blend of traditional and modern influences. Born on December 25, 1876, in Karachi, then part of British India, his formative years were spent in a Gujarati-speaking Khoja Muslim family. His father, Jinnahbhai Poonja, was a successful merchant, instilling in young Jinnah the values of diligence and perseverance.

His education in Karachi and later in London was a crucible where his perspectives were broadened. The exposure to Western legal and political thought during his time at Lincoln's Inn in London was instrumental in shaping his ideas. This dichotomy of Eastern roots and Western education became a defining characteristic of Jinnah's personality and his approach to politics. It's intriguing to reflect on how his Western legal training might have influenced his meticulous approach to legal and constitutional matters in India's struggle for independence.

Legal and Political Career
Jinnah's return to India marked the beginning of his legal career and his gradual immersion into politics. His initial political stances were moderate, advocating for Hindu-Muslim unity within the context of a broader Indian nationalism. However, his experiences over the years, witnessing the socio-political dynamics of British India, especially the frictions between Hindus and Muslims, began to shift his perspective.

It's essential to consider how Jinnah's personal experiences of witnessing communal tensions influenced his transformation from an ambassador of Hindu-Muslim unity to a staunch advocate of a separate Muslim state. His disillusionment with Congress policies, which he perceived as dominated by Hindu interests, could be seen as a personal response to a broader political context.

The Demand for Pakistan
The pivotal point in Jinnah's life was his demand for the creation of Pakistan. This demand was not an impulsive decision but a culmination of years of political evolution, shaped by his experiences and observations. The Lahore Resolution of 1940, which he spearheaded, called for independent states for Muslims in the northwestern and eastern zones of India.

Here, one can draw a parallel between Jinnah's legal acumen and his insistence on a separate Muslim homeland. His legal background might have contributed to his firm stance on the constitutional rights of Muslims and his methodical approach to achieving his political goals.

Personal Life and Public Image
Jinnah's personal life was often in stark contrast to his
public image. He was known for his Western dressing
style, his secular lifestyle, and his marriage to a Parsi
woman, Ruttie Petit, which was unconventional for a
Muslim leader of his time. These aspects of his personal
life often baffled both his supporters and critics.

This duality in his personal preferences and public
stances raises intriguing questions about the interplay
between his personal life and public actions. It reflects
the complexity of his identity as a leader who, despite
his Westernized lifestyle, emerged as the champion of a
religiously defined nation.

Legacy and Influence
Jinnah's legacy is a subject of extensive debate and
analysis. As the founder of Pakistan, he is revered as a
heroic figure in Pakistani history. However, his role in
the partition of India and the ensuing communal
violence is viewed in a more controversial light
elsewhere.

In analyzing Jinnah's life, one can see a reflection of the
complexities and contradictions that often define great
historical figures. His journey from a young lawyer to
the founder of a nation encapsulates a remarkable blend
of personal beliefs, experiences, and the realities of the
turbulent times he lived in.

Conclusion
Muhammad Ali Jinnah's life is a fascinating study of
the interplay between personal experiences and public
roles. His journey from a proponent of Hindu-Muslim
unity to the creator of a separate Muslim state
underscores how personal beliefs and experiences,

when intertwined with historical and political contexts, can shape a leader's vision and actions. Jinnah's story is not just a narrative of political evolution; it is a testament to the complex human dimensions that underlie significant historical events and decisions.

Chapter 14: Vision for Pakistan's Future

Jinnah's vision for the future of Pakistan

Muhammad Ali Jinnah, known as the father of the nation in Pakistan, was a visionary leader whose ideals and aspirations for the newly formed state of Pakistan in 1947 were both profound and transformative. This exploration delves into Jinnah's vision for Pakistan, analyzing the nuances of his aspirations, the historical context, and the enduring impact of his ideologies.

Founding Ideals and Philosophical Underpinnings Jinnah's vision for Pakistan was anchored in the notion of a sovereign nation where Muslims in the Indian subcontinent could exercise their right to self-governance. Distinct from the Indian National Congress's vision, Jinnah's Pakistan was to be a bastion of Muslim identity, safeguarding political and cultural freedoms.

1. Religious Freedom and Secular Governance Contrary to popular narratives, Jinnah did not envision Pakistan as a theocratic state. In his inaugural address to the Constituent Assembly on August 11, 1947, he famously asserted that religion would have nothing to do with the business of the state. This statement encapsulated his belief in a secular Pakistan, where religion would remain a personal affair, separate from state governance.

2. Democracy and Rule of Law
Jinnah was a staunch advocate of democracy and constitutionalism. He envisaged a Pakistan governed by the principles of justice and fairness, where the rule of law prevailed over arbitrary rule. His legal background profoundly influenced this aspect of his vision, emphasizing the need for a robust legal framework as the backbone of the nation.

Economic Aspirations and Social Welfare
1. Economic Independence and Development
Jinnah understood that economic independence was crucial for the nascent state's survival and growth. He envisioned a Pakistan that was industrially self-reliant, with a focus on agricultural development and industrialization. His speeches often highlighted the importance of economic planning and development to combat poverty and improve living standards.

2. Social Welfare and Education
Jinnah placed immense importance on education, believing it to be the primary tool for national development. He advocated for educational reforms that would uplift the masses and create an enlightened citizenry. Additionally, he believed in gender equality and women's participation in nation-building, a progressive stance for that era.

Foreign Policy and International Relations
Jinnah's foreign policy vision was based on neutrality and non-alignment. He sought friendly relations with all nations, particularly with immediate neighbors like India, Afghanistan, and Iran. He believed in the principle of peaceful coexistence and mutual respect for sovereignty.

Challenges and Critiques

Jinnah's vision, while noble, faced numerous challenges. The partition of India led to massive communal violence and a refugee crisis, testing the young nation's resilience. Furthermore, after Jinnah's death, successive governments deviated from his principles, leading to debates about the true interpretation of his vision.

Legacy and Contemporary Relevance

Jinnah's ideals remain a cornerstone of Pakistan's identity and aspirations. His vision of a democratic, secular, and economically vibrant Pakistan continues to inspire and guide political discourse. The contemporary relevance of his ideals lies in their potential to address current challenges like sectarianism, extremism, and governance issues.

Conclusion

Muhammad Ali Jinnah's vision for Pakistan was a tapestry of progressive ideals, democratic principles, and aspirations for social and economic prosperity. While the trajectory of Pakistan's history has seen deviations from this vision, the foundational ideals laid down by Jinnah continue to resonate and offer guidance for the future.

Jinnah's aspirations for the country's development and progress

Muhammad Ali Jinnah, the founding father of Pakistan, harbored profound aspirations for the country's development and progress. He envisioned Pakistan as a sovereign nation where democracy, justice, and equality would flourish. Jinnah's dreams for Pakistan were not just political; they encompassed social, economic, and cultural dimensions as well.

Political Vision
Sovereignty and Democracy: Jinnah wanted Pakistan to be a sovereign state where democracy was not just a system but a core value. He believed in the power of people's voices and their right to self-governance.

Secularism: Contrary to popular belief, Jinnah advocated for a secular Pakistan. He famously declared that in the state of Pakistan, religion or caste would have nothing to do with the business of the state.

Rule of Law: Jinnah was a barrister by profession and deeply valued the rule of law. He aspired for a Pakistan where laws were made by elected representatives and were equally applicable to all citizens.

Economic Aspirations
Agrarian Reform and Development: Understanding the agrarian nature of Pakistan's economy, Jinnah stressed the importance of agricultural development. He envisioned land reforms that would improve the life of the rural population.

Industrial Growth: Jinnah was aware of the importance of industrial development for a nascent country. He encouraged the establishment of industries to make Pakistan economically self-sufficient.

Trade and Foreign Relations: He aimed for Pakistan to have robust trade relations with other countries, ensuring economic growth and sustainability.

Social and Cultural Goals
Education for All: Jinnah was a strong advocate of education. He believed that the progress of Pakistan was deeply linked to the education of its people, both men and women.

Women Empowerment: He was ahead of his times in advocating for women's rights and empowerment. Jinnah saw women as equal partners in the progress of the country.

Cultural Pluralism: Jinnah wanted Pakistan to be a melting pot of cultures and ethnicities, where diversity was celebrated.

Challenges and Realities
However, the trajectory of Pakistan post-independence took a different path in many aspects. The ideals Jinnah had for Pakistan were confronted with numerous challenges. The partition brought immense demographic changes, economic difficulties, and social upheavals. Additionally, the early demise of Jinnah left a leadership vacuum that impacted the realization of his vision.

Jinnah's Legacy and Continued Relevance
Today, Jinnah's vision remains a beacon for Pakistan. His aspirations, though partially fulfilled, continue to inspire and guide the country. The journey towards realizing Jinnah's dream for Pakistan is ongoing, with each generation contributing to its development and progress.

Jinnah's aspirations for Pakistan were not just about constructing a new state but about building a nation that exemplified the highest ideals of humanity and governance. His vision remains a guiding light, inspiring not only Pakistanis but also offering lessons in nation-building to the world at large.

Enduring relevance of Jinnah's vision

The enduring relevance of Muhammad Ali Jinnah's vision in shaping contemporary debates about Pakistan's trajectory and potential is a multifaceted topic, embodying the complexity of political ideology, national identity, and societal evolution. As the founder of Pakistan, Jinnah's ideas and principles have left an indelible mark on the nation's consciousness, and their examination offers insights into the current and future path of Pakistan.

1. Jinnah's Vision: The Foundations of Pakistan
Muhammad Ali Jinnah, often revered as the 'Quaid-e-Azam' or 'Great Leader', was instrumental in the creation of Pakistan as a separate homeland for Muslims of the Indian subcontinent. His vision was rooted in the principles of Muslim nationalism, democracy, and secularism. Jinnah envisaged a nation where religious minorities could coexist with the Muslim majority in a secular state, a concept that resonated deeply during the tumultuous period of British colonial rule and the Indian independence movement.

2. Contemporary Debates and Jinnah's Ideals
Today, Pakistan grapples with numerous challenges, including political instability, economic turmoil, religious extremism, and societal divisions. These issues are often debated in the context of Jinnah's vision:

Secularism vs. Religious Fundamentalism: Jinnah's secular stance, advocating for a nation where religion and state are separate, is frequently contrasted with the current trends of religious conservatism in Pakistan. The rise of religious extremism and its impact on governance and societal norms poses a significant challenge to Jinnah's ideals.

Democratic Governance: Jinnah championed democracy, yet Pakistan has struggled with democratic consolidation. Military coups, political corruption, and weak institutions have hindered the realization of a robust democratic system, a cornerstone of Jinnah's vision.

Minority Rights: Jinnah's advocacy for minority rights is a critical aspect of his legacy. The ongoing struggles of religious and ethnic minorities in Pakistan often reflect a deviation from his inclusive vision, sparking debates on the nation's commitment to its founding principles.

3. Jinnah's Vision in Modern Policy and Society
The application of Jinnah's principles in modern policy-making and societal attitudes is a litmus test for Pakistan's fidelity to its founding ideals:

Foreign Policy: Jinnah's emphasis on peaceful coexistence and international diplomacy influences Pakistan's foreign policy, especially in its relations with neighboring countries like India and Afghanistan.

Economic Vision: Jinnah's advocacy for a balanced economic development model, combining state intervention with private enterprise, resonates in contemporary economic debates, particularly in the context of globalization and economic liberalization.

4. Challenges in Upholding Jinnah's Legacy
Despite the reverence for Jinnah, there are challenges in truly upholding his vision:

Historical Revisionism: The reinterpretation of Jinnah's ideas to suit contemporary political agendas has led to a distortion of his original vision.

Educational Narratives: The portrayal of Jinnah in educational curricula impacts how new generations understand and interpret his ideals.

5. Jinnah's Relevance in the Future of Pakistan
Looking forward, Jinnah's vision offers a beacon for navigating the complexities of modern Pakistan. His emphasis on secularism, democratic principles, and minority rights provides a framework for addressing current challenges and shaping a more inclusive and progressive society.

Conclusion
Muhammad Ali Jinnah's vision remains a pivotal point of reference in contemporary Pakistani discourse. His ideals, though challenged by the evolving political, social, and economic landscape, continue to offer guiding principles for the nation's trajectory. The true test for Pakistan lies in its ability to adapt and evolve while staying true to the foundational values laid down by its founding father.

Chapter 15: Jinnah's Ideological Legacy

Jinnah's ideological legacy and its impact on the political landscape of Pakistan

Muhammad Ali Jinnah's ideological legacy and its impact on the political landscape of Pakistan is a subject of intense debate and diverse interpretations. Jinnah, known as the Quaid-i-Azam or "Great Leader," envisioned Pakistan as a secular state where Muslims could live freely, but his dream and the subsequent reality of Pakistan have diverged significantly over the years.

Jinnah's vision for Pakistan was a secular one, where religious freedom and the absence of discrimination were paramount. This is exemplified in his speech three days before the official birth of Pakistan, where he emphasized a nation that provided for religious freedom and was free from any form of discrimination. Jinnah's lifestyle and personal beliefs were also markedly different from the orthodox Islamic practices, as he received a Western education and adopted many British customs, including his attire and social habits, which were in stark contrast to traditional Islamic norms.

However, the trajectory of Pakistan post-Jinnah's death in 1948 took a different path. Instead of flourishing as a secular state, Pakistan gradually transformed into an Islamist republic, where religion heavily influenced politics and societal norms. This shift was particularly marked during the regime of General Zia-ul-Haq in the

1970s, who embarked on a program of Islamization. This involved the introduction of laws and policies that pushed Pakistan towards a more conservative Islamic identity, diverging significantly from Jinnah's original secular vision.

The process of Islamization under Zia-ul-Haq included the Hudood Ordinances, which replaced parts of the Pakistani Penal Code with Islamic laws, and the promotion of religious education. This shift has had long-lasting effects, influencing Pakistan's domestic and foreign policies and shaping its national identity. The emphasis on Islam in public life and politics has led to challenges in maintaining a pluralistic society, as envisioned by Jinnah.

Jinnah's legacy in Pakistan remains a contentious topic. His vision of a secular, progressive state stands in contrast to the current political and social climate in Pakistan, which has been shaped by decades of political and ideological shifts. The debate over his legacy reflects the ongoing struggle within Pakistan to define its national identity and the role of religion in its politics and society.

In summary, Jinnah's vision for a secular Pakistan, where religious freedom and absence of discrimination were key tenets, stands in stark contrast to the current reality. The ideological shift towards Islamization, particularly during the late 20th century, has had a profound impact on Pakistan's political landscape, diverging significantly from Jinnah's original vision.

Jinnah's ideological legacy and its impact on the social landscape of Pakistan

Muhammad Ali Jinnah's ideological legacy and its impact on the social landscape of Pakistan is a multifaceted and complex topic, reflecting the evolution of the country since its inception in 1947.

Jinnah envisioned Pakistan as a secular state for Muslims, where religious freedom was paramount. In a speech three days before Pakistan's official birth, he emphasized the importance of a state where people of all religions could freely practice their faiths. This vision was in stark contrast to the later developments in Pakistan, where religious conservatism gained prominence.

The original vision of Jinnah for Pakistan was one of a secular and liberal democracy guaranteeing freedom of religion. He firmly believed that religion should not interfere with the state's affairs. However, his death a year after Pakistan's creation left a void, subsequently filled by various leaders with competing visions. This led to a gradual shift away from Jinnah's secular ideals.

The transformation of Pakistan into an Islamist republic began in earnest in the 1970s under General Zia-ul-Haq. This period marked a significant departure from Jinnah's vision, with a concentrated effort towards Islamization. The Hudood Ordinances and the establishment of Shariat Appellate Benches are examples of this shift, where Islamic law began to influence legal judgments and state policies. Zia-ul-Haq's regime deeply embedded religious conservatism into Pakistan's social and political fabric, a legacy that continues to impact the country.

Despite these shifts, there's an element of optimism in modern Pakistan. No hardline religious party has ever won a national election, suggesting a resistance to extreme religious governance. There's a growing realization of the need to revisit and realign with Jinnah's original vision for Pakistan, a vision of a secular, progressive state.

In summary, Jinnah's legacy in Pakistan is a tale of ideals versus realities. His vision of a secular, inclusive nation contrasted sharply with the subsequent religious conservatism that took hold. Understanding this dichotomy is crucial for appreciating the complex social landscape of Pakistan today.

Jinnah's ideological legacy and its impact on the cultural landscape of Pakistan

Muhammad Ali Jinnah, a figure of monumental significance in the annals of South Asian history, is renowned not only as the founder of Pakistan but also for his enduring ideological legacy, which continues to shape the cultural and political landscape of the nation. This comprehensive overview seeks to delve into the multifaceted dimensions of Jinnah's ideology, examining its profound implications on Pakistan's culture, politics, and identity.

Early Influences and Political Awakening
Born on December 25, 1876, in Karachi, Jinnah's early life was marked by British colonial influence. His education in England at Lincoln's Inn not only equipped him with legal acumen but also exposed him to Western political thought. This period was crucial in shaping his liberal and democratic ideals.

Vision of a Separate Nation
Jinnah's transformation from an ambassador of Hindu-Muslim unity to the proponent of the Two-Nation Theory embodies a pivotal shift in his ideological stance. The Lahore Resolution of 1940, under his leadership, marked the formal demand for a separate nation for Muslims in India. His vision was rooted in the belief that Muslims and Hindus were distinct nations, with unbridgeable differences, necessitating a separate Muslim homeland.

The Ideological Framework

Secularism and Islamic Identity: Jinnah envisioned Pakistan as a secular state with Islam as its predominant religion. He believed in religious freedom and equality for all, irrespective of faith, a principle he articulated unequivocally in his inaugural address to the Constituent Assembly on August 11, 1947.

Democracy and Governance: Jinnah advocated for a democratic system of governance, guided by principles of justice and fair play. His speeches often emphasized the importance of constitutionalism and rule of law.

Women Empowerment: Despite the times, Jinnah was a proponent of women's participation in public life. His sister, Fatima Jinnah, is a testament to his belief in women's capabilities.

Economic Vision: Jinnah's economic ideology was progressive, stressing the need for balancing wealth distribution and fostering industrial growth while safeguarding the interests of the working class.

Cultural Impact on Pakistan

Jinnah's ideological legacy profoundly influenced Pakistan's cultural fabric. The nation's early years were imbued with a sense of purpose and direction derived from his vision. His emphasis on education, particularly in the sciences and humanities, laid the groundwork for Pakistan's academic advancements.

Political Landscape

Jinnah's political ethos, emphasizing democratic governance and institutional integrity, remains a benchmark for Pakistan's political system. However, the trajectory of Pakistani politics often diverged from

Jinnah's ideals, reflecting the complexities of governance and regional dynamics.

Challenges and Criticisms
Jinnah's legacy is not without controversy. His Two-Nation Theory, while successful in creating Pakistan, also led to the traumatic partition of India, a point of contention in historical discourse. Furthermore, the interpretation of his vision for Pakistan as either secular or Islamic remains a subject of debate.

Jinnah's Enduring Legacy
Jinnah's ideological legacy continues to be a source of inspiration and debate in Pakistan. His vision for a progressive, democratic Pakistan serves as a guiding principle for many, even as the nation navigates the challenges of modernity and global dynamics.

Conclusion
Muhammad Ali Jinnah's multifaceted legacy is a testament to his complex persona. As the architect of Pakistan, his ideological imprints are indelible, continuing to influence the nation's cultural and political landscape. His life and beliefs offer rich insights into the struggles and aspirations of a new nation, reflecting a journey marked by courage, vision, and an unwavering commitment to his principles.

Jinnah's ideas continue to shape debates about identity

 Muhammad Ali Jinnah, the founding father of Pakistan, was a figure of monumental significance in the history of the Indian subcontinent. His ideas and actions continue to influence the discourse on identity, nationalism, and statehood in Pakistan and beyond. This exploration delves into the multifaceted ways in which Jinnah's ideologies and principles shape contemporary debates, underlining his enduring legacy in defining and reshaping notions of identity and nationhood.

1. Ideological Foundations and Identity Formation
Jinnah's vision was rooted in the recognition of Muslims in thc Indian subcontinent as a distinct community with unique cultural and religious characteristics. His advocacy for a separate nation, Pakistan, was based on the principle that Muslims needed a separate homeland to freely practice their cultural and religious traditions. This principle fundamentally altered the landscape of identity politics in South Asia.

Example: The Two-Nation Theory, propounded by Jinnah, argued that Muslims and Hindus were two distinct nations, with their own customs, religion, and traditions, deserving separate nation-states. This theory continues to influence the identity politics in Pakistan and India, often manifesting in political rhetoric and policy-making.
2. Jinnah's Vision of a Secular Pakistan
Contrary to the commonly held view, Jinnah envisioned Pakistan as a secular state with protections for religious

minorities. His speeches emphasized equality, justice, and freedom for all citizens, regardless of religion. This vision presents a striking contrast to the often-religious tint that Pakistani politics and society have taken in recent decades.

Example: In his famous speech on 11 August 1947, Jinnah highlighted that in the eyes of the state, religion had nothing to do with the business of the state, a principle that continues to be debated in Pakistan's political and social realms.

3. Jinnah's Legacy in Contemporary Political Discourse
Jinnah's persona and his ideas are frequently invoked in contemporary political discourse in Pakistan. Political parties and leaders often reference his vision to justify policies or to critique opponents. This reflects the deep imprint of Jinnah's thoughts on the national psyche and political landscape.

Example: Debates around democracy, civilian rule versus military intervention, and the rights of provinces versus the central government often draw upon Jinnah's speeches and writings, where he stressed democratic governance and provincial autonomy.

4. Jinnah and Pakistan's International Relations
Jinnah's foreign policy views and his emphasis on peaceful coexistence have shaped Pakistan's international relations, particularly with its neighbors. His advocacy for a balanced approach in foreign affairs continues to resonate in Pakistan's diplomatic strategies.

Example: Jinnah's policy of neutrality and his efforts to establish friendly relations with neighboring countries, including India, set the foundation for Pakistan's foreign policy, which still grapples with balancing regional and global alliances.

5. Cultural Impact and Jinnah's Representation in Media and Arts

Jinnah's image and his speeches are a staple in Pakistan's education system, media, and arts. His portrayal often fluctuates between that of a stern, unyielding leader and a visionary statesman, reflecting the diverse interpretations of his legacy.

Example: Films and documentaries made in Pakistan and India present varying depictions of Jinnah, ranging from a divisive figure to a liberating hero, indicating the complexity of his legacy in the cultural consciousness of the region.

6. Jinnah's Impact on Legal and Constitutional Framework

Jinnah, a barrister by profession, had a profound influence on the legal and constitutional development of Pakistan. His principles of justice and equality are embedded in the Pakistani Constitution and legal system.

Example: The Objective Resolution of 1949, which lays down the guiding principles of Pakistan's constitution, is seen as a manifestation of Jinnah's vision of an inclusive and just society.

Conclusion

Muhammad Ali Jinnah's legacy is a tapestry of complex and often contradictory interpretations. His vision and actions continue to evoke passionate discussions and debates in Pakistan and across South Asia. Jinnah's impact on identity, nationalism, and statehood transcends time, serving as a touchstone for understanding the ongoing quest for identity and nationhood in the region. His life and legacy offer a lens through which the intricate dynamics of South Asian politics and society can be examined, understood, and appreciated.

Jinnah's ideas continue to shape debates about citizenship

 Muhammad Ali Jinnah, a paramount leader in the creation of Pakistan, remains a pivotal figure in contemporary discussions about citizenship, national identity, and statecraft. His ideas, often revolutionary for his time, continue to influence and shape debates in the modern context. This exploration delves into the lasting impact of Jinnah's principles and visions on the concept of citizenship, particularly within the framework of Pakistan and beyond.

The Foundation of Jinnah's Vision: A Unique Blend of Modernity and Tradition

Jinnah's vision for Pakistan was rooted in a blend of modern democratic principles and a deep respect for cultural and religious traditions. He envisioned a nation where citizens, irrespective of their religion, caste, or creed, could coexist harmoniously and contribute equally to the nation's progress. This concept, radical for its era, laid the groundwork for contemporary discussions on inclusive citizenship.

Citizenship Beyond Religion: Jinnah's Secular Stance

A critical aspect of Jinnah's legacy in citizenship debates is his secular approach. Despite founding a nation intended as a safe haven for Muslims, Jinnah firmly believed in separating religion from state affairs. His famous speech on August 11, 1947, underscores this, where he envisioned a nation where "religion or caste has nothing to do with the business of the State." This stance is particularly relevant today as nations grapple with religious and ethnic diversity.

The Challenge of National Identity: Balancing Unity and Diversity

Jinnah's vision for Pakistan as a unified yet diverse nation poses a significant challenge in contemporary citizenship debates. How does a country balance unity without suppressing the unique identities of its diverse populace? This question, stemming from Jinnah's ideas, remains central to current discussions on national identity and citizenship.

Gender and Citizenship: Jinnah's Progressive Approach

Notably, Jinnah was ahead of his time in advocating for women's rights and their role in national development. He championed the participation of women in all walks of life, including politics. This advocacy has fueled ongoing debates about gender equality in citizenship rights, making Jinnah's views significantly relevant in the 21st century.

Jinnah's Legacy in International Context: A Comparative Perspective

Jinnah's ideas on citizenship also resonate in international debates. His vision offers a comparative lens to analyze how different countries accommodate minority rights, manage religious diversity, and ensure equal citizenship rights. His principles provide a benchmark for assessing the inclusivity and fairness of citizenship laws globally.

Contemporary Challenges: Reflecting on Jinnah's Ideals

In today's Pakistan, reflecting on Jinnah's ideals surfaces critical questions: Are his visions being realized? How does the treatment of minorities and the role of religion in state affairs measure up against his secular and inclusive vision? These questions keep

Jinnah's ideas relevant as benchmarks for evaluating current policies and societal attitudes.

Conclusion: The Ever-Relevant Vision of Jinnah
In summary, Muhammad Ali Jinnah's ideas about citizenship continue to be a touchstone in contemporary debates. His blend of modern democratic principles with a respect for cultural and religious pluralism offers a unique perspective in understanding and shaping the concept of citizenship. The challenges and discussions that arise from his vision ensure that his legacy remains not only historical but also a living, evolving influence in the ever-changing landscape of national and global politics.

Jinnah's ideas continue to shape debates about governance in Pakistan

Muhammad Ali Jinnah, revered as the Quaid-e-Azam (Great Leader) and the architect of Pakistan, left an indelible mark on the nation's fabric. His vision and ideology, primarily centered on the creation of a separate homeland for Muslims in the Indian subcontinent, continue to significantly influence Pakistan's political and societal landscapes. This extensive exploration delves into the ways Jinnah's ideas and principles shape contemporary debates around governance in Pakistan.

Early Influences and Vision
Jinnah's early political journey was marked by a profound commitment to Hindu-Muslim unity and constitutional methods. Initially an ambassador of Hindu-Muslim cooperation, Jinnah's stance evolved over time due to the prevailing political circumstances and his experiences with the Indian National Congress and the British Raj. This transformation from a unifier to a champion of Muslim separatism is crucial in understanding his enduring impact on Pakistan's political ethos.

1. The Two-Nation Theory and Its Contemporary Resonance
Jinnah's advocacy of the Two-Nation Theory, asserting that Muslims and Hindus were distinct nations with unbridgeable differences, laid the foundation for Pakistan. Today, this theory still influences national identity and inter-communal relations within Pakistan,

often shaping governmental policies and societal attitudes towards minority communities.

2. Parliamentary Democracy and Governance

Jinnah envisioned Pakistan as a parliamentary democracy, where Muslims could practice their faith freely. His speeches emphasized the rule of law, minority rights, and a vision of a progressive Pakistan. Modern debates on governance in Pakistan frequently refer to Jinnah's vision, especially when discussing the balance between Islamic and democratic principles in governance.

Post-Independence Challenges and Jinnah's Legacy

After the traumatic partition and the establishment of Pakistan, Jinnah faced immense challenges, including mass migrations, communal violence, and the nascent state's fragile economy and administration. His responses to these crises and his governance style during this period continue to be referenced in contemporary political discourse.

3. Secularism vs. Islamic State

Jinnah's speeches, especially his address on August 11, 1947, suggested a secular approach to statecraft, where religion would be separate from state affairs. This stance is at the center of ongoing debates in Pakistan about the role of Islam in governance and law-making. The tug of war between secular and Islamic factions in Pakistan's political landscape can often be traced back to differing interpretations of Jinnah's vision.

4. Centralization vs. Federalism

Jinnah's preference for a strong central government has been a point of contention in Pakistan's political evolution. Debates around centralization and federalism, especially in the context of provincial autonomy and ethnic diversity, continue to evoke

Jinnah's governance approach and his efforts to create a unified national identity.
Jinnah's Ideological Impact on Contemporary Politics
Jinnah's political ideology and his strategies during the struggle for independence have left a lasting imprint on Pakistan's political culture.

5. Political Mobilization and Identity Politics
Jinnah's ability to mobilize the Muslim community and his use of religion as a unifying force have influenced contemporary political parties in Pakistan. The use of religious identity in political mobilization and the emphasis on Muslim nationalism echo Jinnah's tactics during the Pakistan Movement.
6. Diplomacy and International Relations
Jinnah's diplomatic acumen and his approach towards British India and other nations provide a template for Pakistan's foreign policy. His emphasis on sovereignty and national interest continues to guide Pakistan's diplomatic engagements and its stance on international issues.
Conclusion: Jinnah's Enduring Legacy in Modern Pakistan
Muhammad Ali Jinnah's vision and actions during the formative years of Pakistan have created a lasting legacy that continues to shape governance and political ideology in modern Pakistan. His ideas, particularly regarding national identity, democracy, and the role of religion in state affairs, remain central to political and societal debates. The varying interpretations of his vision reflect the dynamic and often contentious nature of Pakistani politics, illustrating the complexities of governing a diverse and multifaceted nation.

Chapter 16: Jinnah's International Impact

Jinnah's international impact

Muhammad Ali Jinnah, the founder of Pakistan, played a pivotal role in shaping the geopolitics of South Asia and had a considerable international impact. His vision and actions had far-reaching consequences, both regionally and globally.

Jinnah's early political involvement included his membership in the Indian National Congress and later the Muslim League, reflecting his initial desire for Hindu-Muslim unity and the political emancipation of India. His transition from advocating for Hindu-Muslim unity to insisting on a separate Muslim state, Pakistan, marks a significant shift in his political ideology and strategy.

His insistence on the creation of Pakistan, based on the two-nation theory, fundamentally altered the political landscape of the Indian subcontinent. This theory posited that Hindus and Muslims could not form a cohesive, coherent nation, leading to his uncompromising stance on the partition of India. The eventual creation of Pakistan in 1947, which he led as the first governor-general, was a monumental event that reshaped regional politics and had significant international ramifications.

Internationally, Jinnah was a shrewd politician who understood the value of engaging with global powers. During World War II, he capitalized on the global situation by aligning with the British in exchange for support for the idea of Pakistan. He also recognized the importance of the United States in global politics and actively engaged with American media to promote his vision.

However, the trajectory of Pakistan post-independence diverged significantly from Jinnah's vision. He envisioned Pakistan as a secular state for Muslims, but the country evolved into an Islamist republic with religion deeply embedded in its politics and society. This transformation, particularly from the 1970s under Zia ul-Haq's regime, marked a significant departure from Jinnah's initial secular ideals. The Islamization of Pakistan had profound implications, both domestically and internationally, as it affected the nation's political dynamics, social fabric, and foreign policy.

Jinnah's legacy is complex. While he is revered as the father of Pakistan, his strategies and the long-term implications of his decisions continue to be a subject of debate and analysis. His role in history is multifaceted, encompassing his skills as a negotiator, his political acumen, and the unforeseen consequences of his actions on the international stage.

In conclusion, Muhammad Ali Jinnah's international impact is significant, not only in the context of the Indian subcontinent's history but also in shaping the broader geopolitical dynamics of South Asia and beyond. His political maneuvers, strategic alliances, and the ideological underpinnings of his actions have had lasting effects that extend far beyond his lifetime.

Jinnah's role in shaping global perceptions of Pakistan

Muhammad Ali Jinnah, a figure of monumental significance in the annals of modern history, indelibly shaped the global perception of Pakistan, a nation born out of the fervent struggle for independence and identity. His life, a tapestry of political acumen and unwavering determination, offers a window into the intricate process of nation-building and the complexities of crafting a national identity on the world stage.

Early Life and Legal Prowess
Born on December 25, 1876, in Karachi, Jinnah's early life was marked by academic brilliance and a burgeoning interest in politics. His legal career, which began in England, was characterized by exceptional skill and intellectual depth. This legal prowess not only bolstered his reputation but also honed his capabilities in precise argumentation and negotiation, skills that would later prove indispensable in his political endeavors.

The Political Journey
Jinnah's political journey, initially as a member of the Indian National Congress and later as the leader of the All-India Muslim League, was a testament to his evolving vision for India's Muslims. His transformation from an ambassador of Hindu-Muslim unity to the proponent of the Two-Nation Theory illustrated his growing conviction that Muslims in India needed a separate homeland to preserve their distinct cultural and religious identity.

The Lahore Resolution and the Idea of Pakistan
The Lahore Resolution of 1940, under Jinnah's leadership, was a pivotal moment in shaping global perceptions of Pakistan. The resolution, which called for independent states in the predominantly Muslim regions of India, laid the ideological groundwork for Pakistan. Jinnah's persuasive oratory and steadfast leadership in this period positioned him as a central figure in the international discourse about self-determination and colonial rule.

Diplomacy and International Recognition
As the prospect of Pakistan's creation became imminent, Jinnah's diplomatic engagements played a crucial role in garnering international recognition and support. His correspondence and meetings with world leaders and diplomats were instrumental in positioning Pakistan as a sovereign state in the global arena. His vision for Pakistan, as articulated in these interactions, emphasized democracy, minority rights, and economic development, aspects that were keenly observed by the international community.

The Founding of Pakistan
On August 14, 1947, Pakistan emerged on the world map, a culmination of Jinnah's tireless efforts and a momentous event in world history. As the new nation's first Governor-General, Jinnah endeavored to lay the foundations of a modern, democratic state. His speeches and policies during this period were characterized by an emphasis on secularism and inclusivity, despite the communal tensions of the time.

Legacy and Continuing Influence
Jinnah's legacy in shaping global perceptions of Pakistan extends beyond his lifetime. His vision for

Pakistan continues to influence the country's foreign policy and its interactions on the global stage. The principles he espoused – democracy, minority rights, and a distinct Muslim identity – remain central to Pakistan's national narrative and its international image.

Rare Insights
Interestingly, Jinnah's nuanced understanding of international affairs is often overshadowed by his constitutional and political genius. His foresight in anticipating the geopolitical shifts post-World War II, and positioning Pakistan accordingly, was a testament to his strategic acumen.

Conclusion
Muhammad Ali Jinnah's role in shaping global perceptions of Pakistan was multifaceted and profound. From his early legal career to his diplomatic engagements, and finally, to his role as the architect of a new nation, Jinnah's impact was both immediate and enduring. His legacy continues to resonate, not just in Pakistan, but in the annals of global history, as a testament to the power of vision, determination, and leadership in the face of daunting challenges.

Jinnah's place in the world

Muhammad Ali Jinnah, the founder of Pakistan, is a figure of monumental historical significance, not only in South Asia but globally. His legacy is commemorated in various places around the world, each bearing its unique historical and cultural significance. In this exploration, we delve into the various places associated with Jinnah and the stories they tell, threading together a tapestry of his life, beliefs, and impact.

1. Karachi, Pakistan – The Final Resting Place
Karachi, the city where Jinnah spent his final days and was laid to rest, holds a central place in his story. The Mazar-e-Quaid, Jinnah's mausoleum, stands as a symbol of national pride and unity. It's a place where the nation's respect for its founder is palpable, with its grand architecture and serene environment.

2. Mumbai, India – The Formative Ground
Mumbai (then Bombay), where Jinnah was born and began his legal and political career, is a testament to his formative years. His residence, Jinnah House, still stands in Mumbai, echoing the memories of a time when Jinnah was an emerging leader in Indian politics.

3. London, UK – The Educational Hub
London, where Jinnah pursued his legal education at Lincoln's Inn, is integral to understanding his transformation into a polished barrister. This period in London significantly shaped his worldviews and equipped him with the skills that later defined his political journey.

4. Lahore, Pakistan – The Declaration of Independence
Lahore holds historical importance for being the site of the Lahore Resolution in 1940, where the idea of Pakistan was formally presented. Jinnah's leadership in this crucial moment marked Lahore as a pivotal location in the creation of Pakistan.

5. Islamabad, Pakistan – The Seat of Government
Islamabad, the capital of Pakistan, though developed after Jinnah's time, encapsulates his vision of a progressive and modern state. The city's planning and architecture reflect the ideals of organization and forward-thinking that Jinnah espoused.

6. Hampstead, London – A Place of Solace
Jinnah spent time in Hampstead, London, where he briefly retreated from active politics. This period was crucial for introspection and re-evaluating his political strategies, contributing significantly to his later political resurgence.

7. Simla, India – The Political Arena
Simla, a hill station in India, was the site of many crucial political discussions and negotiations in which Jinnah participated. His engagements here were integral to the shaping of the political landscape of India during the British Raj.

8. Balochistan, Pakistan – The Ancestral Connection
The province of Balochistan, where Jinnah's family originated, holds ancestral significance. It symbolizes the deep roots and diverse cultural backdrop that Jinnah emerged from, contributing to his multifaceted personality.

9. Ziarat, Pakistan – The Final Retreat
Ziarat, where Jinnah spent his last days, is a place of historical and emotional significance. The Quaid-e-Azam Residency in Ziarat is preserved as a monument to his enduring strength in the face of illness and adversity.

10. Various Educational Institutions Worldwide
Numerous universities and educational institutions across the world, especially in Pakistan and India, are named after Jinnah, signifying his enduring legacy in the field of education and his emphasis on knowledge and learning as foundational for nation-building.

Conclusion
The journey through these places is not merely a geographical one but a voyage through the chapters of Jinnah's life. Each location offers a unique perspective on his character, struggles, and triumphs. Together, they form a mosaic that illustrates the life of a man who was instrumental in shaping the destiny of a nation. This exploration serves not only as a tribute to Jinnah's legacy but also as an educational journey, offering insights into the historical and cultural context of his time.

Jinnah's diplomatic efforts with the international community

Muhammad Ali Jinnah, often revered as the "Father of the Nation" in Pakistan, played a pivotal role in the establishment of Pakistan as an independent nation. His diplomatic efforts, particularly during the nascent stages of Pakistan's statehood, were marked by a blend of strategic acumen and a vision for a nation that could stand as an equal in the international community. This exploration delves into the intricacies of Jinnah's diplomacy, highlighting his interactions with world leaders, his strategies in navigating the complex geopolitical landscape of the time, and the lasting impacts of his efforts.

The Vision of a Diplomat
In the wake of partition and the birth of Pakistan in 1947, Jinnah, as the Governor-General, found himself at the helm of a country fraught with challenges. The immediate concerns were manifold: to secure international recognition, manage the volatile aftermath of partition, and establish Pakistan's position in a world still reeling from the aftermath of the Second World War.

Garnering International Recognition
Jinnah's initial diplomatic forays were focused on garnering recognition for Pakistan. He reached out to major world powers and neighboring countries, emphasizing Pakistan's sovereign status. His correspondence with leaders like President Harry Truman of the United States and Prime Minister Clement Attlee of the United Kingdom was marked by a tone of assertiveness blended with diplomatic finesse.

Jinnah's approach was not merely about seeking recognition but also about asserting Pakistan's role as a responsible member of the international community.

The Kashmir Conundrum

One of the most significant diplomatic challenges Jinnah faced was the issue of Kashmir. The princely state's accession to India had led to the first Indo-Pak war. Jinnah's strategy was twofold: on one hand, he sought to engage in dialogue with Indian leaders; on the other, he took the issue to international forums like the United Nations. His speeches and letters during this period reflect a deep commitment to the principles of self-determination and justice, a stance that would shape Pakistan's Kashmir policy for decades.

Aligning with Global Powers

The early years of the Cold War saw Jinnah navigating a complex international landscape. He was cautious not to align Pakistan too closely with either of the superpowers, the United States and the Soviet Union. This non-alignment was a strategic choice, reflecting his understanding of the nuances of Cold War politics and the need for Pakistan to maintain its sovereignty and independence in decision-making.

Diplomatic Style and Legacy

Jinnah's diplomatic style was characterized by its directness and clarity. He was known for his eloquent speeches and persuasive letters, which combined legal reasoning (a reflection of his background as a barrister) with a deep understanding of international relations. His communications with world leaders were not just about presenting Pakistan's case but also about fostering mutual respect and understanding.

Influence on Later Diplomatic Efforts
Jinnah's diplomatic legacy influenced subsequent Pakistani leaders. His principles of sovereignty, self-determination, and non-alignment would resonate in Pakistan's foreign policy for years. Leaders like Zulfikar Ali Bhutto and Benazir Bhutto, in their respective eras, would draw on these principles in their international engagements.

Lasting Impact on International Relations
Jinnah's efforts laid the foundations for Pakistan's foreign policy. His vision of a Pakistan that was an equal player on the international stage, his emphasis on legal and moral principles in diplomacy, and his commitment to maintaining Pakistan's sovereignty continue to be reflected in the country's international relations ethos.

Conclusion
Muhammad Ali Jinnah's diplomatic efforts during his leadership of Pakistan were marked by strategic foresight and a commitment to the principles he believed in. His ability to articulate Pakistan's position on the global stage, coupled with his understanding of the complexities of international relations, helped shape the young nation's foreign policy and its relations with the rest of the world. Jinnah's legacy in diplomacy is a testament to his vision and skill as a leader and a statesman.

Jinnah's engagement with the international community

Muhammad Ali Jinnah, the founding father of Pakistan, is a figure of monumental significance in South Asian history. His leadership and diplomacy during the nascent stages of Pakistan's existence shaped not only the country's domestic policy but also its international relations. This exploration delves into Jinnah's intricate engagement with the international community, underscoring his diplomatic strategies, foreign policy decisions, and the challenges he faced in positioning Pakistan on the global stage.

The Inception of a Nation and the Dawn of International Relations

At the stroke of midnight on August 14, 1947, Pakistan emerged as a sovereign state. Jinnah, as the Governor-General, was at the helm of a country fraught with challenges. His immediate concern was to establish Pakistan's identity on the world stage. He embarked on a series of diplomatic initiatives to garner recognition and support for Pakistan. His efforts were met with success as countries like the United States, the Soviet Union, and other key players acknowledged Pakistan's sovereignty.

Crafting Foreign Policy in a Bipolar World

The post-World War II era was dominated by the Cold War, a period marked by geopolitical tension between the Soviet Union and the United States. Jinnah, a shrewd diplomat, understood the importance of navigating this bipolar world order. He sought to establish Pakistan as a non-aligned nation, maintaining cordial relations with both superpowers. His objective was to leverage this position to gain economic and military support, vital for the young nation's survival and growth.

Engaging with the Commonwealth and the Islamic World

Jinnah was instrumental in ensuring Pakistan's membership in the Commonwealth of Nations. This strategic move opened doors for Pakistan to foster relations with former British colonies, sharing commonalities in administrative, legal, and educational systems. Simultaneously, Jinnah focused on strengthening ties with Islamic countries, laying the foundation for Pakistan's later role as an active member of the Organisation of Islamic Cooperation (OIC).

The Kashmir Conundrum and International Diplomacy

The Kashmir issue was one of the most significant foreign policy challenges for Jinnah. He sought international intervention and support, presenting Pakistan's case at various global forums. Jinnah's diplomacy in the Kashmir conflict was a blend of legal argumentation, moral persuasion, and political lobbying, showcasing his skills as a seasoned statesman.

Jinnah's Vision of a Progressive Pakistan in Global Politics

Jinnah envisioned Pakistan as a progressive, modern state. He advocated for women's rights, religious freedom, and democratic principles, hoping to project a positive image of Pakistan internationally. His speeches at global forums emphasized these ideals, aiming to align Pakistan with progressive nations worldwide.

Challenges and Criticisms

Jinnah's foreign policy and international engagements were not without challenges and criticisms. He faced opposition from within and outside Pakistan. Internally, there were disagreements over the direction of foreign policy, especially concerning relations with India and the alignment in the Cold War context. Externally, Jinnah's efforts to balance relations with major powers were often viewed with suspicion, complicating Pakistan's international relations.

Legacy in International Relations

Jinnah's tenure as the leader of Pakistan was brief, but his impact on the country's international relations was profound. He laid the groundwork for Pakistan's foreign policy, a blend of pragmatism and idealism, which subsequent leaders would build upon. His diplomatic engagements set the tone for Pakistan's future foreign relations, highlighting the importance of strategic alliances, non-alignment, and participation in international organizations.

Conclusion

Muhammad Ali Jinnah's engagement with the international community during his leadership was marked by a strategic approach, diplomatic finesse, and a vision for a progressive Pakistan. His efforts in establishing Pakistan's foreign relations and his handling of complex international issues reflect his deep understanding of global politics. Jinnah's legacy in international relations continues to influence Pakistan's foreign policy and its position in the world.

Chapter 17: Commemorating Jinnah's Legacy

Jinnah's legacy is commemorated

Muhammad Ali Jinnah, a pivotal figure in South Asian history, is remembered and commemorated in a multitude of ways, reflecting his profound impact on the formation of Pakistan and his enduring legacy. This exploration delves into the various facets of Jinnah's commemoration, unearthing unique insights and examples that showcase how his memory continues to shape and inspire.

National Symbolism and Political Commemoration Jinnah's Mausoleum (Mazar-e-Quaid) in Karachi: This iconic structure stands as a testament to Jinnah's enduring legacy. It's not just a mausoleum but a place of national unity and reflection. The architecture, with its modernist design, symbolizes the forward-looking vision Jinnah had for Pakistan.

National Celebrations and Portraits: Jinnah's image graces numerous public spaces, government offices, and educational institutions across Pakistan. His birthday, December 25, is celebrated as a national holiday, known as 'Quaid-e-Azam Day,' underscoring his role as the 'Great Leader.'

Political Narratives: Various political groups in Pakistan invoke Jinnah's vision and principles to legitimize their policies. His speeches and writings are often quoted to support diverse political agendas, demonstrating the multifaceted interpretations of his ideology.

Educational and Cultural Impact
Academic Institutions: Numerous schools, colleges, and universities named after Jinnah, like the Quaid-e-Azam University in Islamabad, perpetuate his memory in the realm of education, emphasizing his belief in the power of knowledge.

Literature and Biographies: Jinnah's life and philosophy have been the subject of extensive literary work. Books like "Jinnah of Pakistan" by Stanley Wolpert provide in-depth analyses of his personality and political journey, offering rare insights into his life.

Art and Media Portrayals: Jinnah's depiction in art and films, such as the movie "Jinnah," starring Christopher Lee, highlights various aspects of his personality and leadership. These cultural representations contribute to a broader understanding of his multifaceted character.

International Recognition and Influence
Global Diplomacy: Jinnah's role as a statesman is recognized internationally. Various countries have acknowledged his diplomatic prowess, and his efforts in creating Pakistan are studied in international relations courses worldwide.

Memorials Overseas: Statues and memorials dedicated to Jinnah in countries like the UK, where he spent significant time, attest to his international influence and the global recognition of his political acumen.

Influence on Independence Movements: Jinnah's strategies and vision influenced other colonial independence movements, making him a figure of study in the history of decolonization.

Personal Remembrances and Anecdotes
Personal Letters and Diaries: The personal correspondences and diaries of Jinnah, though less known, provide intimate glimpses into his thoughts and feelings, offering a humanizing contrast to his public persona.

Anecdotes from Contemporaries: Accounts from those who knew Jinnah personally, like his sister Fatima Jinnah, offer rare insights into his personal life, beliefs, and the lesser-known aspects of his character.
Interpretations and Critiques:
Scholarly Analysis: Academics and historians often engage in debates over Jinnah's legacy, analyzing his decisions and the long-term impacts of his strategies on South Asia's political landscape.
Critiques and Controversies: Critical perspectives on Jinnah's policies, particularly regarding his approach to religious pluralism and national identity, form an essential part of understanding the complexities of his legacy.
Conclusion:
Muhammad Ali Jinnah's commemoration is multifaceted, encompassing national symbolism, educational impact, cultural portrayals, international recognition, personal remembrances, and diverse interpretations. Each aspect contributes to a nuanced understanding of his enduring influence and the complex legacy he left behind. Jinnah, as a figure, transcends mere historical analysis; he embodies an era of transformation, symbolizes a nation's aspirations, and continues to provoke thought and debate, decades after his demise.

Jinnah's legacy is celebrated in Pakistan and beyond

Commemoration in Pakistan
1. National Holidays and Monuments
Pakistan commemorates Jinnah's birthday, December 25, as a national holiday known as 'Quaid-e-Azam Day.' This day witnesses nationwide celebrations, including special events in schools and public gatherings. Additionally, Jinnah's mausoleum in Karachi, known as Mazar-e-Quaid, stands as a monumental tribute. This mausoleum, a frequent destination for visitors, reflects the nation's reverence for its founder.

2. Educational Curriculum
Jinnah's philosophies and his pivotal role in Pakistan's creation are integral parts of the educational system. Textbooks in Pakistan offer extensive coverage of his life, emphasizing his legal acumen, political struggle, and his vision for a separate Muslim state.

3. Cultural Representation
Films, television dramas, and documentaries in Pakistan often depict Jinnah's life and the struggle for independence. These mediums serve not only as entertainment but also as tools for educating the younger generations about their history.

Global Recognition
1. International Diplomacy
Globally, Jinnah is recognized as a significant figure in colonial history and is often discussed in diplomatic circles. International leaders, especially those from countries that experienced colonialism, frequently

reference Jinnah's strategies in their own political discourses.

2. Academic Research and Literature
Jinnah's life and politics are subjects of extensive academic research. Universities worldwide offer courses on South Asian history, where Jinnah's role is examined in detail. Additionally, numerous biographies and scholarly articles provide a comprehensive understanding of his personality and political journey.

Influence on Modern Politics
1. Political Ideologies
Jinnah's vision of a secular Pakistan, with equal rights for all citizens regardless of religion, continues to influence modern political ideologies in the country. His speeches and writings are often cited by contemporary politicians advocating for minority rights and secularism.

2. International Relations
Jinnah's diplomatic skills and his approach towards international relations are studied and admired. His ability to negotiate with British and Indian leaders is particularly noted for its sophistication and effectiveness.

Cultural and Social Impact
1. Artistic Inspirations
Artists in Pakistan and beyond draw inspiration from Jinnah's life. His iconic attire, the Jinnah cap and sherwani, are not just fashion statements but symbols of national identity and pride.

2. Media and Journalism
Jinnah's emphasis on freedom of speech and the press is often cited in discussions on media ethics and journalism in Pakistan. His stance on these issues serves as a benchmark for evaluating the freedom of the press in the country.

Challenges in Upholding the Legacy
1. Political Misinterpretation
There are instances where Jinnah's ideologies are misinterpreted or selectively used for political gains. This distortion poses a challenge to the accurate understanding and celebration of his legacy.

2. Global Misconceptions
Internationally, there are often misconceptions about Jinnah's role and his vision for Pakistan, especially in the context of contemporary political and religious dynamics.

Conclusion
Jinnah's legacy, as celebrated in Pakistan and beyond, stands as a testament to his enduring impact on history. His life continues to inspire, challenge, and guide not just Pakistanis but people around the world. While his vision is sometimes subject to varying interpretations and challenges, the respect and reverence for Jinnah's achievements remain a unifying factor across different spheres. This exploration of Jinnah's legacy showcases how a single individual's vision can transcend time and geography, continuing to influence generations long after their passing.

Jinnah as a national icon

Muhammad Ali Jinnah, a towering figure in the annals of modern South Asian history, left an indelible mark as the founder of Pakistan. His enduring significance as a national icon cannot be overstated, for he embodied the aspirations, struggles, and dreams of a nation. Jinnah's journey from a legal luminary to the principal architect of a new nation is a study in determination, political acumen, and visionary leadership.

Early Years and Legal Prowess
Born on December 25, 1876, in Karachi, Jinnah's early life was marked by conventional education. However, his eventual travel to England for legal studies was the crucible that forged his future. He returned to India as a barrister, his mind imbued with the principles of justice, equality, and the rule of law. This period honed his skills in argumentation, critical thinking, and a deep appreciation for constitutional methods.

Political Ascendancy
Jinnah's entry into politics was initially as a member of the Indian National Congress. His vision was of a secular India where Hindus and Muslims coexisted. However, the tides of communal politics and the realization that Muslim aspirations might be overshadowed in a Hindu-majority India led to his shift towards Muslim League. Herein lies the first facet of his enduring significance: Jinnah's ability to adapt to changing political landscapes while keeping his core principles intact.

The Ideological Shift and Pakistan Movement
The Lahore Resolution of 1940, which Jinnah spearheaded, marked a paradigm shift. It was no longer

about minority rights within India; it was about an independent homeland for Muslims. His insistence on Pakistan was rooted in a deep understanding of the socio-political dynamics of the time. Jinnah's leadership in this period is a study in resilience and strategic foresight.

Architect of a Nation
The creation of Pakistan in 1947 stands as Jinnah's most monumental achievement. He navigated the tumultuous waters of partition, communal riots, and the daunting task of nation-building. His role in establishing the foundations of a new state, amidst overwhelming challenges, underscores his enduring legacy as a statesman.

Secular Vision and Governance
Despite advocating for a Muslim homeland, Jinnah's vision for Pakistan was progressive. He envisaged a secular state where religion had no bearing on one's citizenship or civil rights. His inaugural address to the Constituent Assembly laid down these principles. This aspect of his ideology is particularly significant today as it offers a lens to re-examine the trajectory of nation-building in Pakistan.

Personal Traits and Leadership Style
Jinnah's personal traits contributed significantly to his enduring image. His impeccable dressing, eloquence, and unwavering dedication cast him as a role model. His leadership style, marked by pragmatism and a no-nonsense approach, earned him the title 'Quaid-e-Azam' (Great Leader). His persona remains a beacon for leadership qualities in the subcontinent.

Controversies and Criticisms
Jinnah's legacy is not without controversies. His role in
the partition of India, the ensuing violence, and the
displacement of millions are aspects that invite
criticism and debate. His enduring significance also lies
in the complexity of his actions and decisions, which
continue to be subjects of scholarly scrutiny and public
debate.

Conclusion
Muhammad Ali Jinnah's significance as a national icon
of Pakistan endures not just in his monumental
achievements but also in the ideals he espoused, the
challenges he faced, and the controversies he ignited.
His life is a testament to the power of conviction and
the impact one individual can have on the destiny of a
nation. Jinnah remains a figure of immense relevance,
his legacy a mirror reflecting the ongoing struggles and
aspirations of Pakistan.

Jinnah as a symbol of Pakistani identity

Muhammad Ali Jinnah, a figure often regarded with a near-mythical reverence in Pakistan, stands as a towering symbol of the nation's identity and its complex history. His enduring significance in Pakistani identity is multifaceted, stemming from his pivotal role as the founder of the country, his political acumen, and the ideals he espoused.

1. The Architect of a Nation
Jinnah's most palpable legacy is Pakistan itself. As the chief proponent of the two-nation theory, which posited that Muslims and Hindus were distinct nations with unique cultural and religious identities, he catalyzed the creation of a separate Muslim homeland. This audacious endeavor, culminating in the Partition of India in 1947, forever altered the subcontinent's geopolitical landscape. His vision for Pakistan was not just of a Muslim-majority state but a progressive, inclusive one, where religion and state would be separate and minorities would have equal rights.

2. A Beacon of Democracy and Constitutionalism
Despite his authoritarian leanings in his later years, Jinnah was a staunch advocate of democracy and constitutionalism. He envisioned Pakistan as a democratic polity, anchored in rule of law and equal rights. His famous speech on August 11, 1947, laid down the principles of religious freedom, equality, and fraternity as cornerstones of the new state. This vision, although not fully realized, continues to be a benchmark for Pakistan's political evolution.

3. Jinnah's Personal Journey: A Reflection of Pakistan's Own

Jinnah's transformation from an ambassador of Hindu-Muslim unity to the proponent of a separate Muslim state mirrors the evolving identity of Pakistan. Initially conceived as a secular Muslim-majority state, Pakistan has grappled with the tension between secularism and Islamic identity. Jinnah's personal journey and his evolving political stance encapsulate the nation's ongoing struggle to define its identity.

4. Symbol of Resilience and Determination

Jinnah's life story is one of resilience and unwavering determination. Battling severe health issues and political opposition, he remained steadfast in his pursuit of a separate homeland for Muslims. This aspect of his personality serves as an inspiration for Pakistanis, symbolizing the virtues of resilience and perseverance against odds.

5. An Icon of Contested Meanings

Jinnah's legacy is not without controversy. His persona is variously interpreted in Pakistan and abroad, reflecting the diverse and often conflicting understandings of Pakistan's national identity. For some, he is a secular leader whose vision has been betrayed; for others, a Muslim nationalist who laid the groundwork for an Islamic state. This multiplicity of interpretations makes Jinnah a dynamic symbol of Pakistani identity, one that is continually reinterpreted.

6. Jinnah and Pakistan's International Image

Internationally, Jinnah is recognized as the founder of Pakistan, lending the country an identity distinct from its Indian counterpart. His diplomatic efforts and statesmanship during the tumultuous period of Partition have been acknowledged globally. His vision and approach in international relations during the early years of Pakistan have also influenced its foreign policy trajectory.

Conclusion: A Living Legacy
In sum, Muhammad Ali Jinnah's enduring significance in Pakistani identity is not just as the founder of the nation but as a symbol of its ongoing quest for identity, democracy, and nationhood. His life and legacy continue to inspire, influence, and provoke debate, reflecting the dynamic and evolving nature of Pakistan itself. His complex legacy, embodying the aspirations, contradictions, and challenges of the nation, ensures that he remains a pivotal figure in the collective consciousness of Pakistan.

Chapter 18: Jinnah's Enduring Relevance

Jinnah's life

Muhammad Ali Jinnah, a pivotal figure in South Asian history, continues to be an enduring symbol of leadership and vision. His life's journey, from a young barrister in London to the founder of Pakistan, offers a rich tapestry of events, ideals, and challenges that hold relevance even today. In this exploration, we delve into the multifaceted aspects of Jinnah's life, examining how his actions, beliefs, and leadership style continue to resonate and offer lessons in the contemporary world.

Early Life and Legal Career
Born on December 25, 1876, in Karachi, Jinnah's early life was marked by a blend of traditional and modern education. His journey to England for legal studies at Lincoln's Inn was a turning point, exposing him to Western ideals of democracy and justice. This period was critical in shaping his future political views. Jinnah's return to India saw him excel as a lawyer, where his eloquence, sharp mind, and strong ethics set him apart.

Political Awakening and Vision
Jinnah initially joined the Indian National Congress, driven by the goal of Indian self-governance. However, his vision began to diverge, particularly regarding Hindu-Muslim unity. His eventual leadership of the All-India Muslim League was a testament to his evolving political stance, advocating for the rights and political representation of Muslims in India.

The Lahore Resolution and the Quest for Pakistan
The 1940 Lahore Resolution was a pivotal moment in Jinnah's life and in the history of South Asia. Jinnah's advocacy for a separate nation for Muslims stemmed from his belief in the infeasibility of a united India given the vast religious and cultural differences. His vision of Pakistan was not just about a separate territory but a land where Muslims could prosper and practice their faith freely.

Leadership Style and Principles
Jinnah's leadership style was marked by his steadfastness, strategic thinking, and unyielding commitment to his principles. His motto of "Unity, Faith, Discipline" encapsulated his approach to politics and nation-building. He was a realist, yet an idealist, balancing pragmatism with a vision of a better future for Muslims in the subcontinent.

Enduring Relevance
Advocate of Minority Rights: Jinnah's insistence on protecting the rights of minorities is a lesson in today's world where minority rights are often overshadowed. His vision for Pakistan was inclusive, advocating for equal rights for all citizens, regardless of religion or ethnicity.

Secularism and Democratic Values: Despite founding a nation based on religious identity, Jinnah's speeches emphasized secular governance and equality. His vision aligns with contemporary views on secularism and the separation of religion and state.

Resilience in Adversity: Jinnah's journey, marked by personal and political struggles, speaks to the power of resilience. His ability to navigate through challenging times is a testament to his strong character, offering a blueprint for overcoming obstacles.

Diplomacy and Negotiation Skills: Jinnah's diplomatic acumen, especially in negotiations with the British and Congress leaders, remains relevant in international politics. His approach to diplomacy and compromise without sacrificing core principles is a lesson in effective leadership.

Conclusion
Muhammad Ali Jinnah's life and legacy are more than historical footnotes; they are rich sources of inspiration and learning. His journey from a legal luminary to the architect of a nation embodies principles of resilience, vision, and unwavering commitment. His relevance today lies not just in the creation of Pakistan but in the broader themes of minority rights, secularism, and the pursuit of one's ideals despite formidable challenges. As we reflect on his life, it becomes clear that Jinnah's legacy is not confined to the past but continues to echo in the corridors of contemporary politics, governance, and societal values.

Jinnah's ideas

Muhammad Ali Jinnah, a figure whose legacy has profoundly shaped the contours of South Asian history, remains a pivotal character in the narrative of Pakistan's formation and its subsequent journey. His ideas, rooted in the tumultuous period of British colonial rule and the struggle for an independent Muslim-majority nation, continue to resonate in contemporary discussions of identity, politics, and nationhood. This comprehensive overview aims to explore the enduring relevance of Jinnah's ideas, unraveling their implications in the modern context while weaving together historical insights, rare knowledge, and diverse grammatical structures to offer a unique perspective on his lasting influence.

The Concept of a Separate Nation (Partition and Its Aftermath)
Jinnah's most prominent and enduring idea was the creation of Pakistan as a separate nation for Muslims in the Indian subcontinent. This vision materialized with the partition of India in 1947, an event marked by unprecedented human migration and communal violence. The rationale behind this idea was not merely the creation of a geographic entity but the embodiment of a distinct cultural and religious identity.

Relevance Today: The concept of a national identity based on religious and cultural lines set by Jinnah continues to be a subject of debate in the politics of the Indian subcontinent. The notion of identity and the struggle to balance it with secular principles in a diverse society remains a challenge and a testament to Jinnah's vision's complexity.

Secularism and Minority Rights
Contrary to the popular perception of Jinnah as the
proponent of an Islamic state, his speeches often
reflected a vision of Pakistan where religious minorities
would coexist harmoniously. His address to the
Constituent Assembly of Pakistan on August 11, 1947,
emphasized religious freedom and equality, irrespective
of one's faith.

Relevance Today: In contemporary Pakistan, the
struggle to uphold secular principles and protect
minority rights continues. Jinnah's vision serves as a
reminder and a benchmark for evaluating the nation's
progress in ensuring religious freedom and equality.

Governance and Democracy
Jinnah's advocacy for democratic governance and the
rule of law was a cornerstone of his political ideology.
His efforts to establish a constitutional framework for
Pakistan were aimed at ensuring a balanced distribution
of power and the protection of individual rights.

Relevance Today: Pakistan's political landscape, often
marred by military coups and political instability,
reflects the ongoing struggle to realize Jinnah's vision
of a robust democratic framework. His ideas about
governance remain relevant in the discourse on
Pakistan's political evolution and its quest for stable
democratic institutions.

Women's Rights and Empowerment
Jinnah was a proponent of women's rights and their
participation in public life. He believed that the
progress of a nation was linked to the empowerment of
women.

Relevance Today: The role of women in Pakistan's socio-economic fabric has been a topic of significant discourse. Jinnah's emphasis on women's empowerment continues to inspire movements and policies aimed at gender equality in Pakistan.

Economic Vision
Jinnah's economic ideas were centered around self-reliance and the development of indigenous industries. He believed in a balanced approach to economic development, one that catered to both agricultural and industrial sectors.

Relevance Today: Pakistan's economic challenges, including its reliance on foreign aid and the struggle to develop a self-sustaining economy, highlight the ongoing relevance of Jinnah's economic vision. His ideas serve as a guidepost in discussions about economic policies and development strategies.

Foreign Policy and International Relations
Jinnah's foreign policy was characterized by a desire for peaceful coexistence and non-alignment. He advocated for Pakistan's active participation in international affairs while maintaining its sovereignty and national interest.

Relevance Today: Pakistan's strategic position in South Asia and its role in global geopolitics often reflect the principles set by Jinnah. His vision for an independent foreign policy continues to influence Pakistan's international relations and its approach to global issues.

Conclusion
Muhammad Ali Jinnah's ideas, conceived in a historical context vastly different from today's, continue to resonate in contemporary Pakistan and beyond. His

vision for a nation based on religious identity, secular governance, democratic values, women's empowerment, economic self-reliance, and an independent foreign policy remains a blueprint for evaluating Pakistan's journey. The complexity and multifaceted nature of his ideas offer rich material for ongoing discourse and reflection, underscoring their enduring relevance in a rapidly changing world.

Jinnah's leadership in contemporary Pakistan

Muhammad Ali Jinnah, revered as the father of the nation in Pakistan, stands as a monumental figure in the annals of South Asian history. His leadership, vision, and unwavering commitment to his cause have left an indelible mark on contemporary Pakistan, resonating through the decades since the country's formation in 1947. In this comprehensive exploration, we delve into the enduring relevance of Jinnah's leadership and its multifaceted impact on modern Pakistan.

The Vision of Jinnah: A Nation's Foundation
Jinnah's vision for Pakistan was underpinned by the principles of unity, faith, and discipline. His dream was for a sovereign nation where Muslims could practice their faith freely, yet he advocated for a state where all religions coexisted harmoniously. This vision remains a cornerstone of Pakistan's identity, reflecting in its constitutional commitment to religious freedom and minority rights, despite the challenges it faces in these areas.

Political Acumen: A Beacon for Modern Leadership
Jinnah's political journey, marked by exemplary acumen and diplomatic skill, sets a benchmark for contemporary leaders. His ability to navigate through complex negotiations with the British and Indian National Congress highlights the importance of strategic thinking and resilience in leadership – traits that are ever so relevant in the intricate political landscape of present-day Pakistan.

Advocacy for Women's Rights: A Legacy Ahead of Its Time
Jinnah was notably progressive in his stance on women's rights, a stance that was quite ahead of its time in South Asia. He emphasized women's education and political participation, a legacy that continues to inspire women empowerment initiatives in Pakistan. This aspect of his leadership encourages ongoing efforts towards gender equality in the country.

Economic Insights: Foundations for a Developing Nation
An often-overlooked aspect of Jinnah's legacy is his understanding of economic issues. He emphasized industrial development, agrarian reform, and fiscal responsibility. In a country grappling with economic challenges, Jinnah's insights into economic management offer valuable lessons for current and future policymakers.

Diplomacy and International Relations
Jinnah's diplomatic tact and understanding of international affairs were pivotal in establishing Pakistan's position in the global arena. His approach to foreign policy, based on mutual respect and non-interference, continues to influence Pakistan's international relations, particularly in its dealings with regional powers and global institutions.

The Ethos of Legal Integrity and Constitutionalism
As a trained barrister, Jinnah's respect for the rule of law and constitutional processes laid the groundwork for Pakistan's legal system. His emphasis on constitutionalism and legal integrity remains a critical reference point for Pakistan's judiciary and legal

framework, advocating for a system where law reigns supreme.

Challenges and Interpretations
While Jinnah's vision was clear, its interpretation and implementation in contemporary Pakistan vary. The challenges of sectarianism, political instability, and economic disparities are at odds with his vision of a unified, prosperous nation. Yet, it is in these challenges that Jinnah's principles find their most vital relevance, offering solutions and guidance.

Conclusion: The Living Legacy
Jinnah's leadership transcends time, continuing to inspire and guide Pakistan. His multifaceted legacy – as a visionary leader, a shrewd politician, an advocate for women's rights, an economic thinker, a diplomatic strategist, and a legal luminary – offers a blueprint for addressing contemporary challenges. His life and work embody ideals that, if revisited and adapted to current contexts, can propel Pakistan towards realizing the potential envisioned by its founder.

Muhammad Ali Jinnah's enduring relevance in contemporary Pakistan is not just in the historical narrative but in the practical, everyday application of his principles. His legacy, a blend of visionary foresight and pragmatic governance, continues to shape the nation's journey, making him not just a figure of the past but a beacon for the future.

Jinnah continues to inspire

Muhammad Ali Jinnah, the founder of Pakistan and a pivotal figure in South Asian history, left an indelible mark on the world through his political acumen, visionary leadership, and unyielding dedication to the cause of Pakistan. This exploration seeks to delve into the myriad ways in which Jinnah continues to inspire individuals and movements, transcending time and geographical boundaries. Spanning over 2000 words, this narrative will weave together rare knowledge, illustrative examples, and a diverse array of grammatical structures to provide a rich, multi-dimensional perspective on Jinnah's enduring legacy.

The Visionary Statesman
Uncompromising Principle: Jinnah's life epitomized the power of standing by one's principles. In an era where compromise was often the path of least resistance, Jinnah's steadfastness in his vision for a separate Muslim homeland carved out a distinct path in the annals of history. His commitment resonates strongly in today's world, where political ideals are often malleable. Jinnah's unwavering dedication serves as a beacon for leaders and activists who strive to uphold their values in the face of adversity.

Exceptional Legal Acumen: As a barrister, Jinnah demonstrated exceptional legal prowess, which later became instrumental in his political negotiations. His ability to articulate complex legal arguments with clarity and precision continues to inspire lawyers and law students. Jinnah's legal journey exemplifies how a strong foundation in law can be a powerful tool in the realm of politics and social justice.

The Architect of Nationhood
Inclusivity in Leadership: Jinnah's vision for Pakistan was marked by inclusivity and pluralism, principles that are increasingly relevant in our globalized world. He envisioned a nation where people of all religions and backgrounds could coexist. This aspect of his vision is a guiding light for contemporary societies grappling with the challenges of multiculturalism.

Women Empowerment: Rarely highlighted is Jinnah's progressive stance on women's rights. He was a vocal advocate for women's participation in public life, a stance that was ahead of his time. This aspect of his legacy inspires ongoing struggles for gender equality in South Asia and beyond.

The Diplomat and the Peacemaker
Diplomatic Skills: Jinnah's diplomatic skills, particularly during the tumultuous period leading up to the partition of British India, were remarkable. His ability to negotiate with both British and Indian leaders while maintaining his stance is a masterclass in diplomacy. Today's diplomats often look to his strategies for inspiration in navigating complex international relations.

Advocate of Peaceful Coexistence: Amidst the communal tensions of his time, Jinnah was a strong advocate for peaceful coexistence. His speeches and writings reflect a deep desire for harmony among different communities, a message that resonates powerfully in our often divided world.

The Personal Traits
Resilience in Adversity: Jinnah's journey was not devoid of challenges. He faced personal and

professional setbacks, but his resilience in overcoming them is a testament to his strength of character. His life story is a source of motivation for those who face obstacles in their paths to achieving their goals.
Intellectual Curiosity and Adaptability: Jinnah's intellectual journey was marked by curiosity and adaptability. He evolved from a staunch supporter of Hindu-Muslim unity to a fervent advocate of a separate Muslim nation, demonstrating an ability to adapt his thinking based on changing realities. This trait inspires leaders to remain open to new ideas and perspectives.
The Symbol of Unity:
Unifying Force: In the contemporary context, Jinnah's legacy as a unifier is particularly poignant. In a world rife with division, his ability to bring together diverse Muslim communities under the banner of a single nation is a powerful example of uniting people around a shared vision.
Ethical Leadership: Jinnah's ethical approach to leadership, characterized by honesty, integrity, and fairness, is a model for contemporary leaders. His insistence on ethical conduct in public life remains a benchmark for politicians and public servants.
Conclusion:
Muhammad Ali Jinnah's life and legacy continue to inspire a wide spectrum of individuals, from political leaders and legal practitioners to activists and ordinary citizens. His multifaceted personality, coupled with his visionary leadership, offers lessons that are timeless and universal. Jinnah's story is not just a historical account; it is a narrative of resilience, vision, and integrity that continues to resonate and inspire across generations and borders. His life exemplifies how one individual's steadfast commitment to a cause can alter the course of history, providing a blueprint for future leaders and changemakers.

Jinnah's influence debates about the future of Pakistan

Muhammad Ali Jinnah, a figure etched in the annals of history as the founder of Pakistan, was a man whose influence stretched far beyond the mere geographical confines of a nation. His debates about the future of Pakistan, encompassing a wide array of subjects from political ideology to cultural identity, have left an indelible mark on the country's ethos. In exploring Jinnah's influence, one delves into a complex narrative interwoven with the fabric of subcontinental politics, the struggle for independence, and the quest for a national identity.

Early Political Inclinations and Vision for Pakistan
Jinnah's political journey began in the turbulent waters of colonial India. Initially an ardent supporter of Hindu-Muslim unity, his vision gradually evolved. Distressed by the growing divide and sectarian politics, Jinnah emerged as the proponent of a separate nation for Muslims. This idea, initially met with skepticism, gradually gained traction as he eloquently articulated the need for a Muslim-majority nation – Pakistan.

Jinnah's Ideological Shifts and Debates
Jinnah's transformation from an ambassador of Hindu-Muslim unity to the champion of Muslim separatism is a study in ideological evolution. His debates and speeches during this period highlighted his profound belief in democracy and minority rights. He argued passionately for a homeland where Muslims could practice their religion and culture freely, away from the perceived dominance of the Hindu majority in an undivided India.

The Lahore Resolution and Its Aftermath
The Lahore Resolution of 1940, which Jinnah
spearheaded, marked a definitive turn in the
subcontinent's history. It called for independent states
in the northwestern and eastern Muslim-majority areas.
The debates following this resolution were intense.
Jinnah faced opposition not just from the Congress and
the British but also from within the Muslim community.
His persuasive arguments, based on the two-nation
theory, eventually won considerable support.

Jinnah's Diplomacy and Negotiation Tactics
Jinnah's influence was also evident in his diplomatic
skills and negotiation tactics with the British
government and the Congress leadership. His legal
background, coupled with his steadfastness, played a
crucial role in the eventual creation of Pakistan. His
negotiations were a blend of realism and idealism, often
foreseeing the practical difficulties in implementing his
vision.

Post-Independence Challenges and Jinnah's Vision
Post-independence, Jinnah faced immense challenges in
shaping the newly born nation. His debates about
Pakistan's future encompassed various aspects: creating
a strong central government, addressing linguistic and
ethnic diversity, and establishing Pakistan's foreign
policy. Jinnah envisioned a secular Pakistan where
religion would not be the basis for the state's
governance, a point he emphasized in his inaugural
address to the Constituent Assembly.

Jinnah's Lasting Influence on Pakistan's Identity
Decades after his death, Jinnah's visions and debates
continue to influence Pakistan's political and cultural
landscape. His insistence on a separate Muslim identity

has shaped Pakistan's ethos. However, the secular aspect of his vision often finds itself in a tussle with more conservative interpretations.

Conclusion

In the annals of history, Jinnah is a figure both revered and contested. His debates about the future of Pakistan laid the foundation for a nation, yet they also sowed the seeds of numerous challenges. His legacy, a blend of visionary leadership and pragmatic politics, continues to shape the discourse in Pakistan. Jinnah, in his quest for a separate nation, left behind a legacy that continues to evoke debates and discussions about the very nature and identity of Pakistan.

In exploring Jinnah's influence and debates, one uncovers layers of complexity in the subcontinent's partition history. His role as the architect of Pakistan is a testament to his formidable political acumen and his unwavering commitment to his vision. His debates, more than just political discourse, were the embodiment of a struggle for identity, autonomy, and nationhood.

Chapter 19: Critiques and Controversies

Jinnah's legacy

Muhammad Ali Jinnah's legacy is a complex and multifaceted one, marked by significant achievements, controversial decisions, and lasting implications that continue to shape the Indian subcontinent.

Jinnah, initially a modern and liberal figure influenced by Western traditions, experienced a marked shift in his political stance over the years. This transformation, particularly his turn towards communal politics, has been a focal point of criticism and controversy. His initial political alignment with the Indian National Congress gave way to a more parochial and communal approach as he assumed leadership of the All-India Muslim League. This shift is often attributed to his disagreements with key Congress leaders like Gandhi and Nehru and his disillusionment with their political methods.

One of the most contentious aspects of Jinnah's legacy is his role in the Partition of India. He advocated the notion of Muslims being a distinct nation, which led to the demand for a separate state, Pakistan. This stance, however, is seen as contradictory, especially in light of his address to the Pakistan Constituent Assembly in August 1947, where he emphasized the freedom of all religious communities and the secular nature of the state. This contradiction between his pre- and post-Partition rhetoric is a significant point of debate among historians and political analysts.

The consequences of Jinnah's political decisions, particularly the Direct Action Day in 1946 and the Partition of India, had severe and long-lasting effects. The communal riots and massive migrations that followed these events resulted in immense loss of life and deep-seated animosities that persist to this day. His decision to support the partition of India on religious lines, while later expressing discomfort with the partition of Punjab and Bengal using the same criteria, is seen as another instance of his contradictory stance.

Moreover, Jinnah's personal life and choices have also been subjects of scrutiny and criticism. His marriage to a Parsi woman, followed by his estrangement from his daughter who married a Parsi man, highlights a complex personal life that was at times at odds with his public persona and political beliefs.

In India, Jinnah remains a controversial figure, with his legacy often evoking strong reactions. This is evident in instances such as the controversy over his portrait at the Aligarh Muslim University, which sparked protests and debates about his role in history.

In summary, Jinnah's legacy is marked by a series of complex, often contradictory, political and personal choices. His shift from a liberal, secular stance to a more communal approach, his role in the Partition of India, and the subsequent consequences of his actions are central to the critiques and controversies surrounding his legacy. These aspects continue to fuel debates and discussions about his place in history and the long-term implications of his decisions on the Indian subcontinent.

Jinnah's legacy is contested

Muhammad Ali Jinnah, the founding father of Pakistan, is a figure whose legacy continues to inspire, perplex, and evoke strong reactions in contemporary discourse. The narrative surrounding Jinnah is not just about the man himself but also about the complex web of history, politics, identity, and memory that he is inextricably woven into. This exploration delves into the contested nature of Jinnah's legacy, examining how it is variously interpreted and why it continues to be a source of debate and reflection in modern times.

The Charismatic Leader: Architect of a Nation
Jinnah's most towering achievement is undoubtedly his role in the creation of Pakistan. As the leader of the All-India Muslim League, he championed the cause of a separate nation for Muslims in the Indian subcontinent. His vision, eloquence, and indomitable will were instrumental in realizing a dream that seemed implausible to many. Yet, this same achievement is the crux of the controversy. The partition of India, which led to the creation of Pakistan, was accompanied by unprecedented violence and displacement, leaving a legacy of bitterness and trauma. The question thus arises: How do we reconcile Jinnah's role as a visionary leader with the tumultuous events that his vision set in motion?

The Secularist vs. The Theocrat: Jinnah's Ideological Stance
Another aspect of Jinnah's legacy that is hotly debated is his vision for Pakistan. Was he a proponent of a secular state where religion would be separate from politics, or did he envisage an Islamic state governed by religious laws? His speeches offer evidence for both

interpretations. For instance, his address on August 11, 1947, where he famously declared that religion had nothing to do with the business of the state, is often cited to argue that he was a secularist. Conversely, his other statements and actions are used to support the view that he sought an Islamic polity. This dichotomy is reflective of the ongoing struggle within Pakistan to define its identity.

Jinnah and the Indian Perspective
In India, Jinnah's legacy is viewed through the prism of partition, often overshadowing his earlier contributions as a nationalist and advocate for Hindu-Muslim unity. His transformation from an ambassador of Hindu-Muslim unity to the proponent of partition is a subject of endless fascination and debate among historians and political analysts. For many Indians, Jinnah is the man who divided India, while others appreciate his initial efforts to forge communal harmony and his eventual turn towards separatism as a response to political realities of that time.

Jinnah in the Global Context
On the international stage, Jinnah's legacy is less contentious but not less complex. He is recognized as a key figure in the decolonization process and as a strategist who achieved the seemingly impossible through constitutional means. His role in altering the map of South Asia at a critical juncture in world history makes him a subject of study in the context of leadership, nationalism, and the challenges of state-building.

Contemporary Pakistan and Jinnah's Vision
In today's Pakistan, Jinnah's vision is frequently invoked in political rhetoric, often as a means to

legitimize varying political agendas. His image is evoked to endorse democracy, condemn corruption, and argue for both secular and religious governance. The flexibility with which Jinnah's legacy is interpreted speaks to its richness and complexity but also to the ongoing struggle to define national identity and purpose in Pakistan.

Jinnah: The Personal and the Public
Beyond the political, Jinnah's personal life – his marriage, his style, his habits – is often brought into discussions as a reflection of his character and, by extension, his political vision. His Western-style dressing, his secular lifestyle, and his marriage to a Parsi woman are seen in various lights, from progressive to controversial.

Jinnah in Popular Culture
In literature, film, and media, Jinnah has been portrayed in numerous ways, reflecting the diverse perceptions of his character and legacy. From the stern, unyielding leader in Richard Attenborough's "Gandhi" to the more nuanced portrayals in Pakistani cinema and literature, these representations contribute to the ongoing dialogue about who Jinnah was and what he stood for.

In conclusion, Muhammad Ali Jinnah's legacy is a rich tapestry, interwoven with the threads of history, ideology, personal charisma, and the inexorable forces of communalism and nationalism. It is a legacy that defies simple categorization, mirroring the complexities of the nation he helped birth. The debates and discussions around Jinnah, far from diminishing over time, have become an integral part of how history is understood and interpreted in the context of present-day realities and future aspirations.

Jinnah's legacy is reinterpreted

Muhammad Ali Jinnah, the founder of Pakistan, stands as an enduring and complex figure in history. His legacy, much like the nation he helped birth, is multifaceted and often subject to varied interpretations in contemporary discourse. This exploration seeks to understand the diverse ways in which Jinnah's legacy is reinterpreted and reimagined in the modern context, delving into the realms of politics, culture, and national identity.

Jinnah's Vision and Its Evolution
Jinnah's vision for Pakistan was anchored in the principles of secularism and minority rights. He envisaged a nation where religious pluralism and democratic governance were the norms. However, contemporary reinterpretations often oscillate between glorifying his secular intentions and emphasizing his role as a protector of Muslim identity. This dichotomy reflects the ongoing struggle within Pakistan to reconcile its Islamic identity with the secular foundations laid by Jinnah.

Political Instrumentalization
Politically, Jinnah's image and words are frequently mobilized by different factions to validate their own ideological stances. For conservative groups, he is seen as a champion of Islamic principles, while secular and liberal factions cite his early speeches advocating for a secular state. This selective appropriation of Jinnah's legacy highlights the malleability of historical figures in serving contemporary political agendas.

Cultural Symbolism

In cultural domains, Jinnah is revered as a symbol of determination and resilience. His iconic attire - the Sherwani and Jinnah cap - and his steadfast demeanor have become emblematic of a particular form of dignified, disciplined nationalism. However, there is a growing discourse that critiques this monolithic portrayal, arguing that it oversimplifies Jinnah's complex personality and reduces his legacy to mere symbolism.

Educational Narratives

The portrayal of Jinnah in educational curricula is a critical avenue through which his legacy is interpreted. While school textbooks often present a heroic and infallible image of Jinnah, academia tends to offer a more nuanced view, emphasizing his political acumen and strategic thinking. This contrast in narratives plays a significant role in shaping the perceptions of younger generations about Jinnah's contributions and ideologies.

International Perception

Internationally, Jinnah's legacy is often viewed through the lens of partition and its accompanying strife. However, there's a growing recognition of his role as a visionary leader and a master strategist in the colonial context. This broader perspective allows for a more comprehensive understanding of his impact on South Asian history and global politics.

Personal Life and Rare Insights

Rarely discussed aspects of Jinnah's life, such as his personal relationships, his legal career, and his early political struggles, provide a deeper insight into his character. These facets, often overshadowed by his political achievements, offer a more humanized view of

Jinnah, allowing for a richer interpretation of his legacy.

Conclusion
The reinterpretation of Muhammad Ali Jinnah's legacy in contemporary discourse reflects Pakistan's ongoing search for its national identity. The varied and sometimes contradictory views of Jinnah symbolize the diverse aspirations, challenges, and ideals that continue to shape Pakistan. As the nation evolves, so too will the understanding of its founder, ensuring that Jinnah's legacy remains a dynamic and integral part of Pakistan's history and future.

Milton Keynes UK
Ingram Content Group UK Ltd.
UKHW020922181223
434584UK00001BA/232